When Mothers Pray

Also by Cheri Fuller

When Couples Pray: The Little Known Secret to Lifelong Happiness in Marriage

When Families Pray: 40 Devotions to Build, Strengthen, and Bond

When Children Pray: How God Uses the Prayers of a Child

Opening Your Child's Spiritual Windows

Opening Your Child's Nine Learning Windows

The Fragrance of Kindness: Giving the Gift of Encouragement

My Wish for You: Blessings for Daughters

Quiet Whispers from God's Heart for Women

Trading Your Worry for Wonder

21 Days to Helping Your Child Learn

Teaching Your Child to Write

Motherhood 101

Christmas Treasures of the Heart

Unlocking Your Child's Learning Potential

Extraordinary Kids

Helping Your Child Succeed in Public School

365 Ways to Develop Values in Your Child

365 Ways to Build Your Child's Self Esteem

365 Ways to Help Your Child Learn and Achieve

How to Grow a Young Music Lover

Home Business Happiness

Motivating Your Child from Crayons to Career

HomeLife: The Key to Your Child's Success in School

Creating Christmas Memories: Family Traditions for a Lifetime

A Mother's Book of Wit and Wisdom

CHERI FULLER

When Mothers Pray

Multnomah® Publishers *Sisters, Oregon*

WHEN MOTHERS PRAY

published by Multnomah Publishers, Inc.

Published in association with the literary agency of Alive Communications, Inc.
1465 Kelly Johnson Blvd., Suite 320; Colorado Springs, CO 80920

International Standard Book Number: 1-57673-935-X

Printed in the United States of America

While the events are factual, some names and specific details
have been changed to protect identities.

For information:
MULTNOMAH PUBLISHERS, INC.
POST OFFICE BOX 1720, SISTERS, OREGON 97759

Library of Congress Cataloging-in-Publication Data
Fuller, Cheri.
When Mothers Pray/by Cheri Fuller. p. cm.
Includes bibliographical references and index. ISBN 1-57673-040-9 (alk. paper)
1. Mothers–Religious life. 2. Parenting–Religious aspects–Christianity. I. Title
BV4529.F85 1997 97–17188
248.8'431–DC21 CIP

05 06 07 08 09 – 17 16 15 14 13

To Peggy Stewart and Flo Perkins,

And to the moms and grandmothers who pour out
their hearts in prayer
in the presence of the Lord,
and lift up their hands and hearts to Him
for the lives of their children
and grandchildren
and generations to come

For I will give you abundant water for your thirst
and for your parched fields.
And I will pour out my Spirit
and my blessings on your children.

ISAIAH 44:3, TLB

CONTENTS

FOREWORD

There is a war going on, a spiritual war. The battle is intense and very real. Satan is aggressively trying to steal and destroy our children, families, the nation, and the world. Yet, the Christian has powerful weapons against the powers of darkness. Paul reminds us in 2 Corinthians 10:4, "The weapons we fight with...have divine power to demolish strongholds" (NIV). What are these divine weapons? They are the Word of God, prayer, and Jesus' name. *When Mothers Pray* is about moms using these divine weapons. This book powerfully proclaims the victory that is ours when we pray. The stories shared are about women who don't just read about prayer, listen to tapes on prayer, go to seminars on prayer, but who pray. They believe the promise in Jeremiah 33:3, "Call unto me and I will answer you and tell you great and unsearchable things you do not know." These women stand in the gap for others, knowing their prayers make an eternal difference.

This is one of those rare books you just cannot put down because it brings hope and a deeper love and trust in the Lord. I'm so thankful God placed this book on Cheri's heart. He knew she would capture the praying hearts of moms and be able to transfer those hearts to paper. Her own passion, zeal, and commitment to prayer give great credence to the message. Cheri took this assignment from Him seriously and accurately penned the miracles of God to pass on the legacy of His faithfulness, omnipotence, sovereignty, and goodness in answering His children's prayers. It spills out on every page.

The hearts of the moms in this book so touched me that I laughed, cried, was inspired, blessed, encouraged, and convicted—sometimes all at the same time. As I read the book, I was fasting and praying for one of my children. Many of the scriptures and quotes so comforted me that I would stop and have a quiet time right then. As the Holy Spirit would speak to my heart, I would say, "Yes, Lord, that is the scripture I need right now," and I would write the verse in my journal in the section for a particular child and then pray for him accordingly. The book also contains timeless prayer principles and illustrations that I journaled, as well as personal things of which the Holy Spirit convicted me. It was not only a sweet learning time but a burden-releasing time as well.

Cheri brings our sisters in Christ around the world closer to us. She reminds us that our hearts are the same for our children and that many of us are walking similar prayer journeys. Truly, all over the world there is a chorus "pouring out our hearts like water before the face of the Lord, lifting our hands toward Him for the lives of our children" (Lamentations 2:19).

I appreciated her encouragement that we don't have to carry our burdens for our children by ourselves. Moms In Touch groups provide a safe, loving, confidential atmosphere where burdens become lighter, fears are released, comfort is found, love for one another's children is fostered, deep friendships develop, and spiritual growth in prayer occurs. As Cheri says so beautifully, "Regular weekly prayer time with other women can bring us out of depression and open up windows of strength and opportunity."

I'm eager for you to read this book, and you will want to read it again and again. It lovingly brings us back to the truth that God's will can be done on earth just as it is in heaven, if we will but pray. John Wesley is frequently quoted as saying, "God will do nothing on earth except in answer to believing prayer." Who will stand in the gap for our children, families, schools? Who will pierce the darkness with their fervent, persistent prayers? Will you? If you are not praying for your children, who is?

Gracious, loving, heavenly Father,

May every person who reads this book take seriously the greatest privilege, responsibility, and command we have as Christians: to pray, not just when we feel like it, but even when we don't. May You use this book to ignite the hearts of mothers around the world to seek You, believe Your promises, and stand in the gap for their children. May moms know the Holy Spirit's assurance that their prayers make an eternal difference. May this book provide the needed strength and courage for each mom to raise her children in the love and admonition of the Lord and not give up. May tens of thousands of Moms In Touch groups begin as a result of mothers choosing to take time out of their busy schedules to give their children the gift of their prayers. May each mom know that God will answer the impossible if she will but ask. May You use this book for Your honor and Your glory.

Satan does not want this book read, for he knows that if the weakest saint gets on her knees, he is defeated. Therefore, protect it and place it in the hands of every person You want to read it. May each mom know that she is not alone in her battle and that she is on the winning side. Encourage her heart in knowing that You love her and will never leave her nor forsake her.

In Jesus' powerful, precious name I pray,

Amen—Yes!

FERN NICHOLS
Founder and President,
Moms In Touch International

ACKNOWLEDGMENTS

This book had to be written on my knees, that is, with much prayer! And it couldn't have been completed without the prayer support of many people. So I want to thank all those who labored in prayer for this project. I especially thank Fern Nichols, founder and president of Moms In Touch International, for her inspiration, for her tremendous role model as a faithful mom and intercessor, and for her help in connecting me with mothers who wanted to share the awesome things God has done in their lives through prayer. Thank you to the Moms In Touch International staff, especially Kathy Gayheart, Debbie Khalil, and Jan Peck, for all your help and prayers along the way.

God is always seeking intercessors, but He seems especially intent on rallying them to pray at this particular time in history. As emphasis on prayer has increased, many prayer campaigns have been launched: AD 2000, the National Day of Prayer, Two by Two Thousand, Campus Crusade's Days of Prayer and Fasting, and others. Another part of this prayer movement is the thousands of mothers praying, and that's why I refer to the ministry of Moms In Touch International throughout this book. For decades women have joined in prayer chains and groups to lift their concerns to God. But I believe Moms In Touch, where two or more moms meet for one hour each week to pray in one accord for their children and schools, is one of the most powerful ways God is equipping an army of intercessors to pray for children and youth in America and in over ninety countries in the world today.

I thank you precious women, both in the United States and around the world, who shared your testimonies of what happened when you prayed for your children, and I thank God for your faithfulness in prayer. Many thanks for dear friends who prayed for me: prayer partners of many years Flo Perkins and Peggy Stewart, Cathy Herndon, Cynthia Morris, Melanie Hemry, Susan and John Munkres, our House Church, Linda

Merrick, Barbara Bourne, Phama Woodyard, Barbara James, Susan Stewart, and fellow writers Louise Tucker Jones, Lindsey O'Conner, and Becky Freeman. To Connie Willems, thank you for your insights, questions, and help in the thinking and writing process.

I'm grateful for the wonderful editing skills of Carol Bartley. Thank you, Carol, for your enthusiasm for this project, your insights, and encouragement on this book; I appreciate you. And my heartfelt thanks goes to the Multnomah publishing staff and Don Jacobson for sharing this vision of the tremendous things that happen when mothers pray! Thanks to Greg Johnson of Alive Communications for his support for this book.

I'm thankful for the legacy of prayer passed on to me by my mother, Mildred Heath Wynn, as she modeled a faithful life of intercession for her six children and many grandchildren. Shortly before she died in 1982, she told me, "After praying to the Lord for all of you these many years, now I'll get to see Him face to face and talk to Him about you up close!" Thanks, Mama, for your prayers!

I'm indebted to my family for their loving care always, but especially during book-writing deadlines. To Justin and Tiffany, Alison, and Chris—what a joy it is to pray for you and watch the incredible things God does in your lives! I'm honored to be your mom, and I love you.

And truly, this book wouldn't have been written without the help of my husband, Holmes. Thank you for praying with me and for me, listening to chapters, giving helpful input, loving me, bringing me Chinese takeout at night, and every kind thing you do. You are the *best*.

Answered prayer...makes praying a thing of life and power.
It is the answer to prayer which brings things to pass,
changes the natural trend of things,
and orders all things according to the will of God....
It is the answer to prayer
which makes praying a power for God and for man,
and makes praying real and divine.
What marvelous power there is in prayer!
What untold miracles it works in this world!
What untold benefits does it secure to those who pray!

E. M. BOUNDS

CHAPTER ONE

A MOTHER'S HEART...

OR THAT MONSTER-MOTHER THING

Hannah answered and said, "No, my lord,
I am a woman oppressed in spirit...
I have poured out my soul before the Lord...
I have spoken until now
out of my great concern and provocation."
1 SAMUEL 1:15–16

I couldn't believe what I was hearing. "We've done all we can do for your son." The doctor's words played over and over in my mind. Justin was supposed to start first grade today, not be in serious condition in the hospital....

I got off the phone with our twenty-year-old, knelt by my bed, and wept. Alison had been discouraged for weeks, couldn't sleep, and felt totally unsupported in her new location. "I feel so alone. I can't connect with anyone here..." Her voice broke, and all I heard was her crying. Yet she was six hours away—too far to hug or comfort—and my heart ached for her....

When our son Chris signed up for the Eastern Religion class at the university, I wasn't surprised. Chris had always been a seeker, but he wasn't seeking in campus Bible study groups...not now at least. What "truths" would he be hearing? What if he turned his back on his faith?...

Your fragile child is seriously ill—again.

Your shy, tender-hearted daughter is away from home—adrift and all alone.

Your bright, inquisitive son is learning to think for himself—but looking for guidance in all kinds of places.

Sound familiar? Has your heart ever ached so strongly for your child that you seriously wondered if it might rip apart? As moms, no matter what stage of mothering we're in—experiencing the delight and fear of being responsible for that first, fresh-from-heaven newborn, or wandering around in our empty nests—we are concerned for our children. We hold them when they're sick, ache when they're lonely and lack friends, worry when they struggle in school and even more so when they rebel and make bad choices. We want to protect and nurture and guide these children we literally carried for nine months.

A recent movie reminded me of how strong this mother love is. In *Safe Passage* a mother of seven boys is watching her fourteen-year-old, Percy, play in a school football game. Decked out in his green and white uniform, Percy clutches the football and races toward the goal line. Just as his mom yells from the bleachers, "Look out!" Percy is crushed by a huge linebacker on the opposing team. Knocked unconscious, the boy lies motionless on the field.

Instantly, Percy's mother is on the field with the coach, trainer, and players. She scoops her teenager up in her arms and frantically carries him into the field house as the coach yells, "Wait a minute, Mrs. Singer! We'll get a stretcher!"

Moments later when the doctor brings him to with smelling salts, he asks Percy, "What's your name?"

"Percival Singer," he answers.

"Who is this?" the doctor asks.

Surprised to see his mom in the field house, "My mother," he responds.

"She's a pretty strong lady. She carried you all the way off the field herself," the doctor continues.

"She what! In front of the guys?...like a baby?" Percy asks, shocked and humiliated. He then turns to his mother. "How could you?" he asks. "Why didn't you just leave me there?"

"I'm sorry, I just couldn't help it," she answers. "When a woman becomes a mother, there's this little part of her, this monster-mother thing, that grows and grows, like the things in your cereal box that grow to three hundred times their size. When a woman becomes a mother, it just rules her life—this monster-mother, three-hundred-times bigger part. I saw you lying there. I was scared. I wanted to get you to help. And I couldn't hear or see anything else!"

Her answer is one most of us moms can readily identify with. This "monster-mother thing," this mother-bear instinct, begins emerging the first day we become a mother, and absolutely takes over when one of our kids is hurting or needs help. In truth, this powerful mother heart is a gift from a loving God who knows children need lots of love and nurture.

But with powerful mother love comes a world of other, equally powerful emotions engendered by our own flesh and blood—fear, worry, frustration, anxiety, joy, delight, guilt. "Our children bring about intense emotions in our hearts," says Fern Nichols, founder and president of Moms In Touch. "When they are responsive to us and to the Lord it brings joy, peace, harmony—we're on a roll. But when they are not responsive to us and they are not responsive to the Lord, it brings turmoil and anxiety. We feel hurt, betrayed, and excluded."

No matter which stage of the mothering process you're in right now, no matter on which end of the emotional spectrum you find yourself, the question is the same for you and me, for all of us. How do we handle this "monster-mother thing"?

GOD'S ANSWER TO THE "MONSTER-MOTHER THING"

Throughout the Bible God tells us what to do when we are anxious, worried, or distressed, whether it's about our children or any other issue of life. He says:

"Call to Me, and I will answer you, and I will tell you great and mighty things which you do not know" (Jeremiah 33:3).

"Let him have all your worries and cares, for he is always thinking about you and watching everything that concerns you" (1 Peter 5:7, TLB).

"Gather together and pray…while there still is time" (Zephaniah 2:1–2, TLB).

"Arise, cry aloud in the night.… Pour out your heart like water before the presence of the Lord; lift up your hands to Him for the life of your little ones" (Lamentations 2:19).

Let's look at a mother who did just that, for her prayer is not only the first recorded prayer in the Bible by a woman but a pattern of effective prayer I'll be sharing throughout this book.

Like Mrs. Singer, Hannah was greatly distressed, but over a different matter. She deeply desired a child and had been unable to conceive. To make matters worse, her husband's other wife, Peninnah, had borne him several children, and she taunted Hannah for her barrenness, making her pain even greater.

Elkanah, Hannah's husband, loved her, but he couldn't understand her agony. "Hannah, why do you weep and why do you not eat and why is your heart sad?" he asked. "Am I not better to you than ten sons?" Husbands, even loving ones, sometimes don't understand a woman's heart, but God does.

So Hannah went to the temple and poured out her request to God, making a vow that if He would give her a son, she would dedicate him to the Lord all the days of his life. In her great distress, she "prayed to the Lord and wept bitterly." Her groanings were so deep in her heart that her lips moved, but no words came out. Seeing her, the priest Eli accused her of being drunk. Hannah's answer to Eli was, "No, my lord, I am a woman oppressed in spirit; I have drunk neither wine nor strong drink but I have poured out my soul before the Lord." Eli then gave her his blessing and asked the Lord to grant her request. Hannah left the temple, no longer burdened and sad, and the next morning she rose up and worshiped God.

The Lord heard Hannah's prayer and granted her petition. In time, Samuel was born to Elkanah and Hannah, and Hannah nurtured him until he was weaned. Then the time came for her to fulfill her vow and take him to the temple to live and serve God. He was probably no more than three years old. How difficult it must have been for her to let go of her beloved firstborn son, the one she'd prayed and wept for! But as she had trusted God to answer her prayer, so she trusted Samuel into Eli's hands and God's safekeeping, dedicating him to the Lord's service in the temple.

Despite it being God's temple, this was no godly environment. The leadership was weak, and Eli's sons were evil and worthless; "they did not know the Lord." Sin abounded. Yet Hannah left Samuel there for Eli to train.

Each year Hannah stitched little Samuel a robe and took it to him at the temple. I can just see her hemming him in prayer and love, every stitch a prayer—for God's protection and His favor, and for His glory and purpose to be accomplished through her son's life.

What were the results of Hannah's bringing her need to God in prayer and trusting her child to Him? Her sorrow turned to joy. Freedom and blessing abounded. As she dedicated Samuel to God, her heart sang a song of praise which begins with "My heart exults in the LORD." Later God blessed her with three more sons and two daughters. Samuel grew before the Lord, becoming God's chosen spokesperson in a time in history when words and visions from God were rare. God's power and sovereignty protected her son, and God used him in a great way to fulfill His plan. As 1 Samuel 3:19 says: "Samuel grew and the LORD was with him and let none of his words fail."

THE POWER OF PRAYER

Although we may have a hard time imagining relinquishing our children to God's service at age three as Hannah did, we can learn much from this woman and her prayers. Like Hannah, we can't put our children in a protective bubble until they get through childhood and adolescence. We can't control all the forces that try to undo our careful training and nurture. We can't always pick them up, kiss the hurt, and make everything better, especially when they get big enough to be on the playing field. But we can follow Hannah's example by scooping them up and carrying them to Jesus, who loves our children more than we ever could.

God has given us the same powerful resource to bring all our concerns about our children to Him—the power of prayer. When the love of a mother for her child is connected with God's power through prayer, an irresistible force is released that changes people (including us!), situations, schools, and even communities. Our prayers make a highway for God to come and bring His salvation and intervention. In this book you'll read stories of modern-day Hannahs, women in distress, mothers like you who love their children and whose greatest desire is to call forth God's best for their children—and whose prayers are laying the tracks for God's power to come.

The stories cover the span and seasons of a mother's life—from caring for that totally dependent baby, to walking with children through the school years, to being a mom of a college kid (where did the time go?), and even to being a grandmother. These true stories of prayers offered and prayers answered show what a mighty influence our prayers can exert. They will refuel you, encourage you to persevere, and offer hope as we see over and over that when mothers pray, mountains move. The mountain may be a learning problem, drugs or alcohol, a difficult relationship, rebellion, or a medical crisis. No matter. When mothers pray, school and teachers change, prodigals come home, and sometimes the stirrings of revival are seen. And when we pray for our children, we are also changed.

We learn to let go with grace, our anxiety and heaviness are lifted, peace returns. We see God acting among us. We see His faithfulness.

OUR PROBLEMS WITH PRAYER

Does that sound too good to be true? Is your desire to pray tinged with a bit of guilt, some doubt, some anxiety? Perhaps you feel like many other mothers I've interviewed. Maybe you've even asked some of the same questions they did:

- "With my busy schedule—caring for kids, running a household, working in and outside the home, caring for an aging parent, and everything else—how can I find time to really pray?"
- "What do you do when you don't see any results from your prayers? I've prayed for years for my children, but I don't see any change."
- "With all the distractions, how can I keep my thoughts from wandering? Is God really going to listen to me when I have trouble giving Him my undivided attention?"
- "I hear others talk about having a quiet time, but with children at home, my schedule is never the same two days in a row. What can I do to be consistent in prayer?"
- "How can I pray more effectively for my child?"

Being a Martha at heart who juggles several plates at one time, I can relate to these questions. So besides sharing my own struggles and journeys in prayer, I'll share practical suggestions in each chapter to enrich our prayer lives. There are ideas for both Marthas and Marys, for those of us who are busy and easily distracted and for those who find it natural to be still, to know that He is God and sit at His feet.

Some of the stories you'll read have a wonderful resolution, but others are in process—with the "rest of the story" of God's working in situations and lives still to be seen as we persevere in prayer. Although many are accounts of answered prayer, in no way am I suggesting that prayer is a magic formula for getting our hearts' desire. Much about prayer and how

God works is a mystery, but this we know: God invites us to pray. He hears us and blesses us when we pray. He gives us His Word to equip us and guide us in how to pray and what to pray about, and He promises a special effectiveness in praying in agreement with others.

Prayer isn't a secondary thing; it's the most important thing we can do for our children and ourselves, and it will dispense the most blessings. If all that we do as mothers flows out of the fountain of prayer, we will experience grace, joy, and rest in the heart of the Father. It doesn't mean we won't have difficulties, but we will be able to face them with more energy and confidence.

MY PRAYER FOR YOU

My prayer is that the Lord will use this book to encourage you, to enrich your prayer life, and to fill you with hope. May it help you know that just as God met mothers in Bible times like Hannah, as He has heard the prayers of mothers throughout history and across continents, so He is listening to you, desiring to show you His love and power as you come to the throne of grace and call on Him.

Now may the God of hope fill you
with all joy and peace in believing,
that you may abound in hope
by the power of the Holy Spirit.

ROMANS 15:13

The prayer of the feeblest saint on earth
who lives in the spirit and keeps right with God
is a terror to Satan.
The very powers of darkness are paralyzed by prayer....
No wonder Satan tries to keep our minds fussy in active work
till we cannot think in prayer.

OSWALD CHAMBERS

CHAPTER TWO

CONFESSIONS OF A MARTHA

Don't fret or worry.
Instead of worrying, pray.
Let petitions and praises shape your worries into prayers,
letting God know your concerns.
PHILIPPIANS 4:6, THE MESSAGE

I pulled the rough, brown shawl around my head while the children filed in for their Vacation Bible School "Bible Times" session. My broom moved quickly to and fro across the floor as I began to get into my character, Martha, and act out the scene: Jesus and His disciples, on their way to Jerusalem, have stopped at our village and I've welcomed Him into our home. As I bustle around the makeshift house, fretting over the dinner I'm preparing for them, I become more and more frustrated with my sister, Mary. There she is, sitting at Jesus' feet, listening to Him talk while I'm doing all the work!

Wanting some accountability and fair play here, I come up to Jesus and say, "Lord, is it nothing to You that my sister has left me to serve alone? Tell her then to help me, to lend a hand and do her part along with me."

To which He replies, "Martha, Martha, you are anxious and troubled about many things; there is need of only one thing. Mary has chosen the good portion…which shall not be taken away from her" (Luke 10:38–42, AMP).

THE MARTHA SYNDROME

I don't know how much the kids learned, but after doing the impersonation of Martha four times that day, I realized how much I identified with this woman who lived two thousand years ago! It wasn't hard to get into character, to act overly occupied, to get too busy and "distracted with much serving." Fretting, busyness, and all that goes along with Martha's personality—that was me. Playing Mary—now that would have been acting!

From early childhood I've been an energetic doer who's had a hard time being patient about anything. Growing up in the middle of six children, five of us girls, I woke up chatting and went to bed the same way. Silence and solitude were nonexistent. I knelt with my sisters as Mom led us in "Now I lay me down to sleep..." each night, but I didn't tarry there after the "amen."

As a young mother, I often packed too much into the days, just as I packed too much into my suitcase when going on a trip. Besides nursing babies and all that goes with mothering three children, cooking, and keeping house, I was either studying for a graduate degree or, later, teaching or helping my husband in his business. Like Martha, I had so many things to accomplish—the laundry, dishes, cooking, cleaning, and having time to spend with my kids. Prayer time at Jesus' feet? That was part of my days too, but not to the degree I wished. Where was I going to squeeze more time out of my schedule?

I wanted to be a Mary, to be more faithful in prayer, but I certainly wouldn't have classified myself as the most valiant prayer warrior. In fact, when the minister in our church once asked all the intercessors to raise their hands and file into the prayer room, my hand didn't go up and I didn't budge! In my mind, a faithful "pray-er" was someone who had hours to be in her prayer closet or someone who rose at 4 A.M. to have her quiet time. (At that time most days, I felt brain-dead.)

Can you relate? Are you more familiar with a broom closet than a prayer closet? Do you want prayer to be a higher priority but find your schedule keeps getting in the way? Don't feel alone. After talking to hundreds of women about prayer, I have found that their number-one hindrance to prayer is finding or making quiet time for prayer in the middle of hectic days.

Tammera, a mother of four children, had been a registered nurse and worked full-time before her last two children were born. When she realized she couldn't manage working and little ones, she quit to be a stay-at-home mom. "But I find I still can't manage my time," she says. "I'm overwhelmed and, at thirty-seven, have less energy. I never feel I have time for anything, and unfortunately that also includes God at times!"

Many moms I've talked to were critical of themselves, saying, "I'm not managing my days wisely enough to make time to pray," or "I'm not disciplining myself," or "I have wrong priorities." So guilt and self-condemnation pile on top of the time frustration.

If you can relate to any of us moms who struggle with "not having enough time to pray," or the Martha syndrome, let me assure you, there's hope. But first, we need to look a bit closer to see if busyness is the source or side effect of the problem.

GETTING TO THE SOURCE OF THE PROBLEM

Jody grew up in Hong Kong, where her parents were missionaries. At age nine, she was sent to boarding school in England, as were all the missionary children. From then on, she saw her parents only once a year, except for their rare furloughs. She developed a "stiff upper lip" for dealing with life and grew used to handling everything herself without any nurturing from a mom. After she married, she found it easier to be busy and to ignore the emotional needs of her children and husband. As she focused on a conscious level on "getting things done," she didn't have to deal with the emotions underneath that were too painful. She avoided prayer for the same reasons; if she got quiet and alone with God, emotions surfaced that she preferred to keep buried.

For me too, busyness was a symptom of the problem, not the source. When I could be totally honest about prayer, in the back of my mind I wrestled with the nagging question, Is anybody listening?

Did God hear me as an eleven-year-old when I prayed for months for my father? If so, why did he suffer a fourth heart attack and die? After my mom remarried and my two teenage sisters left home, did He see my tears and confusion when our world seemingly felt apart? Was He watching when my close friend died in an accident a year later? When a sister was hit by tragedy? Feeling devastated and abandoned in those years, I struggled with, Are You there, God? Are You there for me?

As a young Christian, my friend Cyndi also had a hard time believing God loved her because she came from a divorced family with a faithless, alcoholic father who could never be depended upon. A youth leader who knew her struggle encouraged her to pray these words every single day: "Lord, teach me that you love me." Cyndi continued praying that prayer each day throughout her twenties and early thirties, until she discovered how much He did, in fact, love her. When God's love became a real anchor, her prayer life changed, as did her ability to face difficulties and crises with more faith in Him.

Like Cyndi, I had a hard time feeling that God loved me. Although I had given my life to Christ as a twelve-year-old, my struggle with doubt haunted my adolescent years and my twenties. I was seeking a closer relationship with God at the same time I was keeping Him at a distance and avoiding a deep prayer life.

I remember clearly the day God's love began piercing my heart. It was the first Sunday my husband and I attended a couples Sunday school class in Waco, Texas. As we were walking down the aisle to find seats, they were singing "There's a sweet, sweet spirit in this place, and I know that it's the Spirit of the Lord."

We had just experienced the loss of a second child—a baby born prematurely—and although no one spoke of it, the pain in my heart was growing. The darkness of life was real, and even though I was trying to stay busy with graduate courses and parenting, friends and activities—anything to keep the darkness at bay—I was seeking the light. I had tried to handle life in my own strength (which is what we do when we can't trust anyone bigger), but found it empty and burdensome.

As we sat in the circle, the couples shared answers to prayer they'd received that week. One couple shared how God had met a financial need, and another how He'd helped them communicate better. Then one husband and wife shared about being in a full parking lot and praying for a parking place—that God immediately provided.

"Praying for a parking place?" I thought. "Bothering God for something so small? Would God even care?" It seemed ludicrous and I was skeptical. Martha certainly didn't ask Jesus to help her in the kitchen as she struggled to feed everyone. Could God really be interested in the details of our lives? This was a challenging thought, and maybe it made me think because at the time I was so removed from consciously praying about my daily concerns.

JESUS' LIGHT SHINES DESPITE OUR BARRIERS

I continued searching for God as we moved to Tulsa, Oklahoma. But there the rest of the rug was pulled out from under me as struggles multiplied: loneliness from not knowing anyone in a new city and being several hundred miles away from family; anxiety about our older son's asthma attacks; my husband's long work hours. After successfully giving birth to our second son, I was now pregnant again and tired from mothering our two energetic, preschool boys.

After months of study for my master's degree, I had recently finished my thesis and passed the oral exams, so I had nothing to keep me really busy, except getting ready for the birth of our third child. I began reading a Phillips translation of the New Testament that my husband had used in a college religion class. Sitting there all alone every day while the boys were napping, I read through Matthew, through Mark, then Luke.

One afternoon while starting the Book of John, I was struck by the words in the first chapter. They were the first words from the Bible I had ever read and memorized as a six-year-old: "At the beginning God expressed himself. That personal expression, that word, was with God and was God, and he existed with God from the beginning. All creation took place through him, and none took place without him. In him appeared life and this life was the light of mankind. The light still shines in the darkness and the darkness has never put it out" (John 1:1–3, PHILLIPS).

As I read those words, His light pierced my darkness. As never before, I saw Jesus as the Living Word. His presence filled the room and my heart. As surely as Jesus spoke to Martha, He began to speak to me through His Word, to answer my deepest questions and meet me in my struggles.

I was on my way home, and I'd seen my Father standing on the road, holding a light out to guide me.

Doubt and skepticism slowly melted in the light of His presence, and I began a daily conversation with the Lord. No, I wasn't experienced at praying, but we were talking again. And He began to take the threads of my life—my concerns for our children, my fears about our oldest son's asthma, my pain over personal losses, my agony for a sister who was self-destructing due to alcoholism, my strains and hurts in our marriage—and weave them into a prayer.

When I would take a baby step toward God by praying about something, He'd answer and I'd see a little more of His faithfulness. It was as if He was saying, "Yes, I'm here. I care. I'm faithful. Keep coming to me"—much as we stretch out our hands to our little ones when they take their first steps.

Within a few weeks Holmes joined me in lifting our concerns to God together. As God answered our prayers, we entrusted more of our lives to Him. Whether our prayers were about our relationship ("Help our marriage, Lord, and let it begin with me" was a frequent prayer) or for guidance in the job choices Holmes had to make, He showed us not only the way to go, but more of Himself.

I had enrolled in the School of Prayer. And although I was just in kindergarten, I had entered the adventure of a lifetime: learning how to hear, communicate with, and follow the Lord. As I read His Word each day, I saw verses that said, "He is close to all who call on him sincerely" (Psalm 145:18, TLB). And I began to realize that God Himself—who loved my children, my husband, and sister even more than I did—invited me to cast my cares upon Him and to pour out my heart before Him in prayer.

I also began to see that God does indeed care about the details of our lives. Job 23:10 assures me, "He knows every detail of what is happening to me"[1] and Psalm 33:15 describes God's watchful care: "He has made their hearts and closely watches everything they do."[2] If God numbered the hairs of my head and knit all the delicate, inner parts of my body together in my mother's womb as Psalm 139 says, and if He tells us to pray about *everything* in our lives, as Philippians 4:6 says, then He cares, even about the details!

Our lives are made up of small matters, says E. M. Bounds, and nothing is too great or too small to be the subject of prayer. "Prayer blesses all things, brings all things, relieves all things and prevents all things. Every thing as well as every place and every hour is to be ordered by prayer. Prayer has in it the possibility to affect everything that affects us."[3]

I wasn't praying for parking places yet, but this Martha was longing to sit at His feet. You can sit at His feet too.

PUTTING FEET TO OUR PRAYERS

Here are some ideas you might consider to turn your Martha into a Mary.

Reflect and write. Consider writing your responses to the following questions in a journal, or discuss them with a trusted friend.

- What barriers keep you from praying?

- How would you have to view God in order to come to Him with expectation and trust when you pray?

If you constantly struggle with knowing God loves you, write the following prayer in your journal or on a small card and place it where you will see it throughout the day: "I want to believe that You love me, and I want to believe Your Word. Would You show me and teach me Your love?"

Deal with distractions. "Distraction is, always has been, and probably always will be, inherent in a woman's life," says author Anne Morrow Lindbergh. "For to be a woman is to have interests and duties, raying out in all directions from the central mother-core, like spokes from the hub of a wheel."[4]

Sometimes when we get quiet, our minds wander to one of those spokes! When mine begins to run to the duties I have that day—the groceries I need to pick up or the phone call I need to make—I jot a note on a pad of paper I keep nearby, and I commit those very needs or duties to God. Then I can go back to prayer. If a burden or worry about someone pops up in my mind, that's a signal to give it to Him. If painful emotions surface, those too can be given to God, and He can help us handle them.

Take a prayer walk. This can help focus our praying, especially if sitting still isn't your cup of tea. Lois, a mother of six boys, takes a prayer walk each morning when her boys leave for school. Her intention is partly exercise but mostly prayer—her goal being to pray for each of her sons, from elementary to college-age, until she's "covered" them for the day. She lifts up each of their names to God with their greatest need that day. And since they know she's praying at that time, they often give her requests: "Mom, please pray that I pass the exam I studied for." "Pray I'll do my best in basketball tryouts."

When a prayer walk isn't possible, merely starting the day by conversing with God helps us continue our dialogue with Him throughout the day. Pray a verse to Him like, "This is the day You've made; give me the grace to rejoice and be glad in it...whatever I face, Lord!" Then look for ways He answers that prayer throughout the day.

Journal your prayers. When my thoughts are tangled, writing my thanksgivings, confessions, and petitions out on paper makes praying more concrete. I know He "hears" these simple "Dear God" letters just as well as my spoken prayers. And I find, when I write out the problems and send them as a prayer, the Holy Spirit is a wonderful Counselor. In fact, He's the best.

Visualize your audience. Maybe you're like my friend Susan who is more visual. When she prays, she likes to picture God on His throne while she comes to rest on His lap. This helps her focus on God instead of her "to do" list.

Or try picturing yourself as a lamb being tenderly cared for by the Lord, Your Shepherd, who leads you to quiet waters and carries you when you're weary: "Like a shepherd He will tend His flock, in His arm He will gather the lambs, and carry them in His bosom; He will gently lead the nursing ewes" (Isaiah 40:11).

Focus with a photo. One day as I sat down in my office to pray before working at my computer, I looked up and saw the photos of my children, husband, nieces, and friends on the bulletin board. There was Chris—now a tall college guy—shrunk down in time and size to the second grade, decked out in his school uniform, his first pair of glasses, and his precious smile. As I looked at each photo and prayed for each person, my heart was touched with their needs, and the tears flowed. That bulletin board has become my Prayer Board, and the photos help focus and bring my consciousness back to prayer. You might want to create a Prayer Board or a Prayer Photo Album to help you spend time praying for each of your loved ones.

Communicate with God in His own words. The Bible is a great vehicle for focusing our communication with the Lord. Praying the psalms or other Bible verses can help us express our deepest thoughts and feelings to

God. As Judson Cornwall says, "The written Word—the Scriptures—and the living Word—Christ Jesus—introduce us to prayer and instruct us in our praying."[5]

Try taking one of these verses and praying it back to God:

- For example, you could pray 1 Peter 5:7, "Let Him have all your worries and cares, for He is always thinking about you and watching everything that concerns you"[6] like this: "Lord, thank you that you are always thinking about me and watching everything that concerns me, and that you *want me* to give you my worries and cares. Here's what I'm burdened about today…"
- Or from Colossians 2:6–7, "Father, just as I trusted Christ to save me, I want to trust You for each day's problems and live in vital union with You. Help me to sink deep roots into You and draw nourishment. Help me to grow in You, Lord, and become strong in the truth."

Lord, life is so busy and I have a hard time being still.
Thank You that You receive me where I am today,
and that I can cast all my cares upon You.

In Jesus' name. Amen.

Prayer is the expression of the human heart
in conversation with God.
The more natural the prayer,
the more real He becomes.
It has all been simplified for me to this extent:
prayer is a dialogue
between two persons who love each other.

ROSALIND RINKER

CHAPTER THREE

PRAY WITHOUT CEASING?

WAS PAUL TALKING TO MOMS OF YOUNG CHILDREN?

Pray without ceasing.

1 THESSALONIANS 5:17

"Pray without ceasing," Paul says? Had he ever talked to a mother with young children? Certainly he never spent a day with my kids when they were small. Would you like to show Paul your schedule and ask him exactly where he'd slot in this "pray without ceasing" activity?

We mothers probably identify more readily with Wendy who has four active children, including twin kindergartners. "I have so little time when I can stop, be alone, and think, let alone pray!" she laments.

Even women with Mary tendencies, who would love to spend hours in prayer, struggle with finding time to devote to it when their children are young. In fact, does any woman feel the need for prayer more and find the time more elusive than the mother of small children?

Since we can't create more hours in the day, mothers of young children need to be creative in finding time and ways to pray. We need to be experts in "praying without ceasing."

PRAYER AS INTEGRATION, NOT SEPARATION

Although it would be wonderful to draw away every day in the early morning or late evening to spend time alone with God—and surely those times will come again—it's not essential for prayer. Prayer isn't limited to a slot in our schedule. It's living in the Lord's presence and being open to Him. Rather than seeing it as time away from our children, we must integrate prayer into our activities with our children—for our sakes and theirs.

"Prayer is a lifestyle of keeping in touch with our best friend, Jesus, sharing our joy with Him and giving Him our burdens," says my friend Cathy. She allows God to direct her throughout every day at home, not just at church, and uses prayer as her steering wheel, not her spare tire. With Cathy, prayer is a moment-by-moment activity. And her children are richer for it.

When her four children were young, if she heard them fighting with each other in the morning, she prayed with them at the door before they left for school. She encouraged them to ask forgiveness and let God cleanse their lives of any words or actions before they went out, so Satan wouldn't have the victory.

One day in particular stands out in her mind. Mark, age seven, and Susan, age nine, were viciously attacking each other (only verbally, thankfully). "Lord, I don't know what to do!" Cathy prayed, confessing her frustration and her need for His help. "Role-play," He seemed to say. So Cathy took Susan and Mark aside and had them switch roles and act out how they were tearing each other down. Quickly, tender-hearted Susan burst into tears. "It's my fault!" she cried, asking both God's forgiveness and her brother's for her harsh words. Mark, however, had no intention of recanting or praying. Rather than forcing him to say what he didn't yet mean, Cathy left him to deal with it on his own. As his anger festered, he grew more miserable by the hour. The atmosphere of the whole house was tense.

Seeing that Mark was digging himself deeper and deeper into a well, Cathy went into his room that evening, put her arm around her willful and unhappy child, and asked Mark once again to pray with her. This wise mother first of all asked him just to tell God how he felt, including all the anger, resentment, and hurt. Then she asked him to ask God to forgive his wrong attitudes toward his sister. And finally she suggested he ask God to make him into the godly young man He desires.

Cathy waited patiently for his answer, and finally he agreed. The minute he finished praying, the warmth of the Holy Spirit came in, and joy returned to Mark and to their home. Susan and Mark each shared something fun that happened at school, and the family enjoyed a peaceful dinner.

That night when Cathy put Mark to bed, he laced his fingers behind his head and spoke with a maturity beyond his years, "Mom, I want to thank you for waiting for me to pray today. It was amazing! God really took my anger and changed my heart!"

Cathy's natural way of bringing God into her children's conflicts and everyday situations unlocked amazing blessings. Little did Cathy realize it at the time, but this particular day was a benchmark in Mark's life. Talking to God about his feelings became a life pattern. Years later as a young adult serving as a counselor in summer camp, Mark, in turn, passed the message on to many young people. Now married and a parent himself, he keeps short accounts and asks forgiveness quickly when he and his wife have harsh words. Cathy's daughter-in-law is grateful to her for the critical lessons she taught Mark as a young boy.

DART PRAYERS

If you feel overwhelmed some days, consider Janis, a mother of eight who also takes in foster infants awaiting adoption. We might wonder how she prays at all, much less "without ceasing."

"Since I am up early for infant feedings, talking to the Lord in these quiet moments works exceedingly well," says Janis. But early-morning prayers are only part of her prayer regimen. To Janis, "pray without ceasing" means to always be prayerful. Her motto is: Whatever situation arises, pray! When a person comes to mind, pray! "Although a specified time for prayer and study of the Word is essential, ongoing prayer is not to be underrated!" she adds.

Her continual prayerful attitude allows her to send up short prayers immediately as a concern arises. Her day is peppered with quick, "dart" prayers like, "Lord, help me respond to this child in a way that pleases You." "Lord, I forgive this person right now, this very instant. And, Lord, please forgive my unforgiving spirit. Create in me a clean heart, and renew a right spirit within me." These dart prayers find their way to God's ear as surely as our longer, more comprehensive prayers.

LOOK FOR OPPORTUNITIES

Part of this "praying without ceasing" is seeing the opportunities for prayer that are part of our daily lives, and trusting God to use those prayers to impact our children.

Phama, the mother of five boys, starts her conversation with God in the morning, even if it's a short prayer time. She continues her prayer throughout the day, when carpooling or washing dishes or cleaning house. If she's ironing clothes, she prays for the boy who wears those jeans or that shirt to church that week. (With boys ranging from eighteen months to thirteen years old, they're growing so fast the wearer changes from month to month.)

When Phama was going to be out of town for a week, she began the practice of "joining hands" with her sons as she prays. She took card stock in different colors and traced around her boys' hands. Then she wrote each boy's name and the verse she was praying for him on his card, punched three holes, and put them all in her prayer notebook.

She prays Psalm 119:9–11 for her oldest, Todd—that he would keep his way pure by living according to God's Word, that he'd seek God with all his heart, treasure His words, and not wander from His commandments. On Kent's hand, she wrote Isaiah 58:8, praying that when he calls the Lord will answer, that God's righteousness will go before him and the glory of the

Lord will be his rear guard. And on she goes through her roster of boys.

Not only does she have a great reminder that makes her prayers more concrete and focused for each child, but her boys are touched by her faithfulness. While she was tracing their hands, they asked what the cards were for. They realized, some for the first time, that their mom was praying for each of them, individually. Even when they are at school and she's home, their hands are joined in prayer.

No opportunity is overlooked in Phama's desire to have God intervene in their lives. Last fall when the avalanche of Christmas catalogs descended on their house, her boys were consumed with keeping running lists of all the things they just *had* to have for Christmas. Even her phone conversations and showers were interrupted by her bright-eyed five-year-old, eager to show her his latest Christmas wishes. He wanted everything he saw!

"Help, Lord!" Phama cried out. "How do I rid our home of this lust over things in order to help my boys appreciate the holy significance of the Christmas season?"

She spent November praying and planning, looking for things they could do during Advent to replace her boys' "gimme" spirit with a giving spirit. They listened to Christmas music in the van, read scriptures behind each of the twenty-five doors of the Advent calendar she had made, and read a Christmas story each evening after a candlelit dinner. But nothing seemed to sink in. Every evening at dinner the boys argued over whose turn it was to light the candles. Hot candle wax spilled on the tablecloth and intrusive fingers. They even fought over who got to read the Advent Bible verses! And to add insult to injury new holiday catalogs showed up daily in their mailbox.

"Lord!" she wailed. "I've tried absolutely everything possible. What's your plan now? How are you going to redeem our Christmas!"

Although Phama thought her boys just weren't getting the "reason for the season," two weeks before Christmas seven-year-old Marc handed his mother a card he had carefully printed, entitled "Jesus' Birthday":

> It's like Jesus is celebrating His birthday. Then Santa Claus and a Christmas tree and lights come to the party, and the tree says, "I am decorated and pretty." The lights come along and say, "I am colorful and bright." Then Santa Claus says, "I am nice. I give presents to children."
>
> Then Jesus says, "Trees die, lights burn out, and toys break, but my gift is ETERNAL."

Phama was deeply touched by God's answer to her prayers. In the midst of the arguments and wish lists and ruined tablecloths, God had accomplished His purposes. He had overridden all the catalogs and chaos and quietly spoken to her son's heart the clear message of Christmas.

AN IMPACT FOR A LIFETIME

Sometimes, like Phama, you may feel your prayers aren't making a difference. But trust that when you pray for your kids, it's never in vain. It's time well spent for eternity. When mothers and fathers pray, no matter where they are or what their life circumstances are, God hears, and their children's lives are influenced forever. If you've ever doubted your prayers were having an impact, you need to hear Bok Soon Choi's story.

Bok Soon grew up in the countryside of South Korea, where her parents were farmers. All nine of the family lived in a very small house of only three rooms. At night everyone slept in the same room to keep warm.

Each morning Bok Soon's mother would get up at four o'clock to go to church and pray for her children for at least an hour. As soon as she returned, the children would hear her singing praises to God while cooking breakfast.

Their father also got up early and sat for an hour to pray for each one of his children. His strong voice awakened them every morning without exception with the prayer: "Lord, my God, You have graciously given seven precious children unto us as gifts. Let us raise each one of them for Your glory. We need Your help and strength in parenting them. Give us Your grace!"

The sound of their parents' prayers and praise to God was their alarm clock.

But as Bok Soon grew up, she decided her parents were too legalistic. She and her siblings couldn't use bad words like the other kids in the village, they were encouraged to memorize Scripture, they had to go to church. Bok Soon wanted to be free from what she saw as "bondages."

When Bok Soon turned nineteen, she was ready to leave home to pursue more education. More than anything she wanted to be a successful woman. At the breakfast table on her last day, her mom said, "I know you want to get a college education and more, but I urge you to remember your God all the time. Please go to church on Sundays to worship Him. Without Him, you are nothing. I am going to pray for you every day that you may not forget God."

Leaving behind her past, Bok Soon went to Seoul, eager to explore big-city life. She was willing to study hard, even if she had to skip church. What was that compared to success? Her first Sunday in Seoul as she headed for the library to study, she heard a church bell ringing, inviting her to church to worship.

"I was going to ignore the sound. But it kept ringing in my ears until I remembered Mom's saying, 'I am going to pray for you every day that you may not forget God.' So I looked for a church and went in."

After the service, a lady came up to Bok Soon and greeted her. Leading this newcomer to the fellowship hall for refreshments, she questioned Bok Soon: "Where are you from? Do you believe in Jesus?"

When Bok Soon said yes, the woman showed her two pictures. One depicted a person sitting on a chair with Jesus at her feet, surrounded by confusion and disorder. The other showed Jesus sitting on a chair, with the person at His feet. Order, peace, balance dominated the picture. "Which describes you better?" asked the lady.

"I could not lie. I knew that I belonged to the first picture," Bok Soon says.

The woman treated Bok Soon kindly and gave her assignments of Bible reading and memorization for the next week. As a result, in one week Bok Soon read Romans and the Gospel of John over thirty times each and memorized many verses. But her life was still in disorder.

One Sunday afternoon soon after, Bok Soon was listening to a preacher discuss the first chapter of John—about Jesus being the light of the world, sent by God to die on the cross for our sin. "I was overwhelmed by His love and care," she says. "I asked for forgiveness of my sin and believed Him and accepted Jesus as my Lord and Saviour. It was an amazing experience. I knew I was a totally different person, as His joy, love, and peace filled my heart."

Then everything Bok Soon had learned about God from childhood became clear and alive, and she began to worship God. More than anything else her desire now was to glorify Him with her life.

"I look back, back to the memory of Mom and Dad's prayers for their children every morning. My parents' prayers have become reality in my heart and in all of my siblings' hearts and lives," she says. Bok Soon and her husband are now directors of Precept Ministries in South Korea, where she also has started Moms In Touch groups, as part of MITI's international ministry to encourage women to gather and pray for their children.

Bok Soon is proof that parents' prayers make a difference in their children's lives.

PUTTING FEET TO OUR PRAYERS

If four in the morning doesn't sound like your ideal prayer time, you might consider some of these other practical ways to "pray without ceasing."

Ask God to provide. If you find little or no quiet time to pray, cry out to God and ask Him to provide it. It's a prayer He loves to answer. Simply say, "Lord Jesus, I want to spend time alone with You. Show me a way, a space of time, a quiet place where I can seek You." Then trust Him to do just that, and look for the openings. Whenever I prayed this prayer as a mother of small children, a little window would open up. My husband would take them out for ice cream or to the park. A friend would invite them over to play with her children. God faithfully provided.

Pray where you are. The vital thing about prayer is "to believe that God can reach us and bless us in the ordinary junctures of daily life.... You see, the only place God can bless us is right where we are," says Richard Foster.[1] He urges us to "carry on an ongoing conversation with God about the daily stuff of life." We can talk to God about what our children are doing, the challenges we face, the ordinary events of our days (yes, even the details); we can give Him our hurts and disappointments, share our joys, and thank Him for victories and blessings.

We all need times alone with God, but when lengthy times of solitude aren't possible, put all your energy into even the brief moments.[2] Let His Word bring inspiration and freshness to your prayers and listen for His voice.

Carry prayer through your day by looking for and asking God for "cues." When you pass your child's school, pray for his teachers. When you wash his sweatshirt, pray He'll be covered in God's protection and love. When you polish her shoes, pray that her feet will take her in God's paths.

Make a prayer calendar. If your prayer concerns outnumber your minutes, divide your concerns up among the days of the week or month. One busy mom I know prays for one fruit of the Spirit to grow in her son's life each day. Monday she prays for peace, Tuesday that patience will grow in him, Wednesday for kindness...and on throughout the week.

Imagine Jesus were to ask you what you most want Him to do for your children at this time in their lives. How would you answer Him? Let that request be your Monday focus. On Tuesday pray for your child's school, for her teachers and her ability to learn. On Wednesday, pray for your child's relationships, both in the family and with friends. Pray for God to prepare a Christian mate for your child, if that is His will. On Thursday, pray for your child's growth—physical, mental, emotional. On Friday, pray for your child's salvation or spiritual growth. If you have others on your heart who don't know Christ, you could add those to your Friday calendar as well.

Certainly we can't pray about everything every day. If you're frustrated about where to focus, ask God: On whose behalf do You want me to faithfully intercede? Allocate a certain day, either weekly or monthly, for each person, and then you can pour your heart into praying for one person at a time.

Pray specifically. Many women express frustration with wanting to pray more specifically than just asking God to bless their children, to help their children be healthy and grow up safely. Here are some areas you could pray for young children. If one strikes you as needful for your child, jot it on an index card and put it on the kitchen counter to remind yourself to lift that request before God daily:

- That he will come to Christ early and love His Word (2 Timothy 3:15)
- That he will grow in wisdom and in favor with God and those people his life will touch (Luke 2:52)
- That as you teach him God's Word, he'll treasure it in his heart and keep his way pure (Psalm 119:9–11)
- That he will know that Jesus is his best friend, that he can walk and talk with Him and develop a love relationship (John 15:15)
- That he will develop godly qualities such as diligence, kindness, honesty, compassion, patience, self-control. Be aware that as you pray for your child to develop these character traits, God may want to mature you in the same ways (Colossians 3:12–14)

Pray through the developmental stages.[3] Again, to pray for every need our children will have over a lifetime can be overwhelming. You might find it helpful to pray specifically for the developmental stages as your children pass through them.

- Infancy through toddlerhood—You can pray that your infant will develop trust and a strong sense of security as he bonds with you especially. As you're rocking him, feeding him, and maybe most of all when you're trying to comfort him in the middle of the night, these prayers can remind you of the critical nature of this precious time together.
- Toddlerhood—You can pray that your children will develop a healthy sense of independence. In these years children begin to see themselves as more distinct from others and are developing a self-concept. Recognizing and appreciating this stage of autonomy may help you react with patience as your two-year-old's favorite word becomes "NO!"
- Early childhood—In these years you might specifically pray for your children to develop a healthy curiosity, to learn to play well with others, to explore and create without a fear of failure.
- School age—From ages seven to ten, the "industry" stage, you might ask God to help your children discover their God-given gifts and talents, to develop a sense of satisfaction and joy in using their skills so that they believe, "I can do this. I have something to contribute." This is also a critical time for the development of their conscience.

Pray for yourself. Even though much of your focus is on your children, and rightly so, you must not forget to pray for yourself as well. Having been entrusted with these new lives, you may find yourself in need of God's perspective and wisdom and help more than ever before. You might pray:

- That you will see your child with the Father's eyes and respond to her with His heart
- That you will see into the windows of your child's heart and discover her needs
- That you will have God's heart to know how to train your child as God intends

- That you will be filled with God's Word, wisdom, and Spirit daily
- That His joy will be your strength so you can find pleasure in every day of these brief years with your children

As we pray without ceasing, we can make a difference in our children's healthy development, their salvation, and their growing in grace. We can ask big things for our kids because nothing is too difficult for God. And we can have the joy of watching Him work in their lives as we colabor with Him in prayer for His will to be done and for Christ to be glorified in their lives.

Lord, thank You for the precious children
You've entrusted to my care. Grant me the grace
to be faithful to pray for them
and to never get too busy to come to You
with their needs and my needs.
I pray for the wisdom to know what's most important in this season
and for Your love to cover all I say and do.

In Jesus' name. Amen.

It is by prayer that we couple the powers of heaven
to our helplessness,
the powers which can turn water into wine
and remove mountains in our own life
and in the lives of others,
the power which can awaken those who sleep in sin
and raise up the dead;
the powers which can raise up strongholds
and make the impossible possible.

O. HALLESBY

CHAPTER FOUR

THE TOUGHEST PRAYER:

THE PRAYER OF RELEASE

"For this boy I prayed,
and the Lord has given me my petition
which I asked of Him.
So I have also dedicated him to the LORD;
as long as he lives he is dedicated to the LORD."

1 SAMUEL 1:27–28

I sat in the old yellow rocker, snuggling my first baby, Justin, to my breast. With a sense of awe I brushed my fingers over his light brown hair that felt like the downy feathers of a baby duck I had one Easter. Dressed in a little blue gown and wrapped in a brand-new, white blanket—a gift from his grandmom—he was nursing and making little gurgling noises. He smelled delightfully baby-fresh after his bath.

I looked around the nursery and recalled how carefully we'd planned it. On our limited budget we'd picked out unfinished dressers and paint from Kmart, methodically alternating bright yellow, lime, orange, and blue drawers to match everything else in our baby's room. (Keep in mind, this was the early seventies.) I'd read that babies need a colorful, stimulating environment, and we certainly wanted to do everything right. A Raggedy Andy doll hung on the wall and a musical mobile dangled over Justin's crib.

I believed breast-feeding would be best for the baby and that a rocker was an ideal place to nurse, so we found a charming rocker for ten dollars at a flea market, reglued the spools, and painted it antique yellow. Then I needlepointed a colorful chair pad, a challenging task since I'd never needlepointed and could be categorized as "sewing disabled." But nothing was too much work for our first little one.

We were careful also about prenatal care. I tried to exercise faithfully, not to gain too much weight, and not to eat too much ice cream (my weakness which had a direct effect on the previous goal). I read enough to discover that the less anesthetic used in the delivery the better it was for the baby. So even though our only city hospital gave all mothers a general anesthetic and used forceps if necessary, I told my ob-gyn doctor that I was learning Lamaze on my own so I could have natural childbirth. Dr. Lindsey was skeptical; none of his patients delivered that way. "Besides," he added, "hospital rules prohibit your husband from being in the delivery room, so you won't have him to coach you in the hardest part."

Nonetheless, we felt sure this was best for our baby. Since there were no Lamaze classes, I got a how-to Lamaze book, and Holmes helped me practice the breathing and relaxing exercises. "I can do this," I thought. "We've got this under control."

WHO'S IN CONTROL?

Indication number one that everything was *not* under control came when my doctor told me I would be delivering a breech-position baby, who could weigh up to nine pounds! Sure enough, on July 31, 1971, after four hours of pushing, I delivered an eight-and-a-half-pound, breech baby boy. Although I certainly wouldn't have planned it that way, the Lamaze method and a lot of determination got me through. We were back on course.

However, my second indication that everything was not under control came nine months later. One afternoon when I laid our decidedly strong-willed son down for a nap, I heard a loud cry. The next thing I knew he was unconscious, his body lying stiffly on the crib quilt. I grabbed him up and desperately patted his back to start his breathing again. Within a few seconds, he began breathing again—and so did I.

This definitely wasn't part of the plan!

Two months later it happened again. So a neurosurgeon put him on medication, which sent my active baby into hyperactivity. After a difficult year, a pediatric neurologist finally diagnosed Justin as having merely a problem called "breath-holding spells," a problem that wise parenting would correct.

My third notice that things were not under my control came when Justin was four years old and began to have severe asthma attacks. A black cloud of medical problems settled over our home. We couldn't go out of town without Justin's getting sick, and we were becoming regulars in the emergency room.

At this time God began to teach me an important principle about relinquishing control and releasing my children to Him.

THE PRAYER OF RELEASE

It doesn't matter what you call it—relinquishment, release, letting go—when the situation demands it or when you sense a nudging to give your child to God, it's a scary proposition and one of the most difficult problems we face in prayer. We moms were made for nurturing our children, not relinquishing them.

You may be thinking, "I've spent years caring for, loving, feeding, and protecting my child, and then God asks me to let go of him? It's too much to ask! It's just too hard!" We expect that someday our daughter will leave for college or for a job across the country, and then we'll release her to God. (We'll promise most anything when it's a long way down the road!) But when our child is younger, when the releasing happens prematurely (in our estimation), it's so much harder. The mere thought of having to release a child to God may even keep us from praying about it.

As one mother explained, "I'm anxious that something bad will happen to my teen and fearful that he will make a stupid choice. That fear keeps me from trusting God and from entrusting him to God."

Leslie could teach us something about release and control. Leslie's daughter, Marlie, was born with a congenital heart defect; she had holes in the walls between the vertical chambers of her heart. From the moment Leslie saw her baby strapped to an echocardiograph to determine the seriousness of her defect, she was frightened and anxious. She grabbed the reins of control as tightly as she could.

At Marlie's three-year checkup, the doctors announced that the defect was not correcting itself as they had hoped. Open-heart surgery was likely. The news ripped Leslie's heart and tied her stomach in knots. Her questions poured out: "How safe is the surgery? What are the risks? What's the survival rate?"

"All surgery has risks," the doctor began. "There are no 100 percent safe procedures…"

Leslie stopped listening. There was a chance Marlie could die; that was all she could hear.

"At first I was too numb to pray, too angry. It wasn't fair. So many other families had perfectly healthy kids and didn't have to face such painful possibilities," says Leslie. Then she questioned God and His motives: "Why her, God? If there's something I need to learn, isn't there a way to make me suffer instead of her?"

During the six weeks they waited for tests to confirm the surgery, Leslie asked everyone to pray for healing as she wrestled with the what ifs and tried to bargain with God for her daughter. And in the midst of her pain, God slowly began to reach this frightened mom.

"I finally reasoned that I wouldn't be able to go into the operating room with Marlie. I'd have to wait while the doctors literally stopped her heart and redirected its function to a machine. I couldn't do the surgery; I certainly wasn't trained in such intricate matters. But these doctors were. They knew what they were doing, and God had directed us to them. Over my own cries for help, I finally heard His voice, saying, 'Let her go. I'll catch her.'

"'Oh God, how can I possibly do that?' I wondered."

It was a tug of war—God pulling on one side, Leslie on the other. "Let her go; I'll catch her," God promised. "I can't...I don't want to lose her...What if you don't catch her?" Leslie responded. Then she realized that her fear grew out of God's absence in her own life. He was trying to reach her. He wanted to be with her—before, during, and after the surgery, if she'd let Him. Although she couldn't guide the doctor's hands during surgery, God could.

Finally God tugged, and she let go and fell into His arms. She realized because He was in control, they would be all right regardless of the outcome. She couldn't handle it alone, but He never intended for her to. He would be with them.

Once Leslie accepted God's control over her daughter's life, a peace came upon her. She was able to function again and face the cardiologist appointment without fear.

The day arrived for them to meet with the doctors. The test administrator examined the echocardiogram, the picture of Marlie's heart, pointing out things on the screen. "That hole is really small. This one looks pretty small too," she said matter-of-factly. Finally she turned to face Leslie and her husband and said, "I'll send this video to your doctor, but it looks to me like she's healed."

The next morning their doctor confirmed her findings with the words, "I don't think she will ever require heart surgery."

Marlie's heart was healed. And so was her mom's.

When Leslie took that difficult leap of faith, God was there to catch her.

WHY LETTING GO IS SO HARD

Let's face it. "Letting go" is perhaps the hardest work of motherhood, and that's why we resist it. It's a relinquishment of not only our child but also of our self-will and our desires for the outcome of the situation. We know that when we give something or someone to God, we don't always get it back.

But as hard as it is, it's critical to examine this issue more closely, because the prayer of relinquishment is one of the secrets of answered prayer.[1] And we're all going to face it. You may run full force into it the first day your child picks up that shiny new lunch pail, walks tentatively out to the larger-than-life yellow bus, and rides out of your gaze to school. Or you may successfully avoid it until the day he loads his pride and joy with all his earthly belongings, flashes you that grin that cost two thousand dollars in orthodontist bills, and drives off for college, never to really come home again.

It happens in stages and also in defining moments.

For me it happened when our firstborn son was six years old.

CLINGING PRAYER

I was standing by Justin's hospital bed, praying earnestly for him. He'd suffered another serious asthma attack, and after twenty-four hours in the hospital with every kind of treatment and medication, he still wasn't responding. Looking at him lying there, white faced and straining for air, my fear escalated.

The doctor called Holmes and me out into the hall to explain that everything which could be done for our son had been done. "Something inside him has to rally if he's going to pull out of this," he said.

"If?...if he's going to pull out?" I'd put so much hope in what the doctor and hospital staff could do to treat his asthma. And I'd prayed my heart out—clinging prayers, insisting what God should do and holding Justin tightly to me instead of opening my hands and trusting Him.

I walked down the hall to the empty chapel and sat down, numb, exhausted, out of reserves. In the stillness of that chapel and the emptiness of my resources, God asked me to pray something different, something very difficult—a prayer of release. He asked me to give our son to Him.

Have you found it easier to entrust your child to God's care when he's healthy and everything is going fine? The risk seems not nearly so great as when a child is extremely ill or in trouble. Like Leslie, I wrestled with the thought, What if God decides to take him home? I'd already lost a baby and my father, so I knew that was a possibility.

But what God calls us to, He also provides the grace for, and He did for me that day in the hospital. As a thunderstorm raged outside, the lights blinked on and off. A huge boom of thunder riveted my thoughts on God—the One in charge of the universe, the maker of heaven and earth, the sea and everything in it, as Psalm 146:6 says. The same God who sends forth lightning and scatters the enemies (Psalm 144:6) can lift His voice and melt the earth (Psalm 46:6). "And I can't release my son to Someone with this much power?" I thought.

In that moment I realized that not releasing Justin to God could thwart the very power that could help him. Confessing my lack of trust to God, I sensed Him saying, "Hope in Me. Trust his life to Me totally."

I bowed my head and prayed from the bottom of my heart, "Father, I forgot that Justin was Your child first and that You made him. I give him back to You, whatever happens today." A warm peace filled my heart and displaced the icy fear.

Although I didn't know it, at the same time, upstairs in the pediatric ward, our son's condition began to improve. By the time I walked into his room a short while later, he was sitting up, breathing normally, his face full of color.

RELINQUISHMENT DOESN'T GUARANTEE THE RESULTS WE WANT

Praying the prayer of relinquishment doesn't mean the person we pray for is always healed, but it does open a door for the power and presence of God to come in and transform the situation.

When Maureen's daughter Emily was seven months old, she suffered a stroke because of a missing artery in her brain. At eleven months another stroke wiped out all the abilities she'd gained thus far. The doctors didn't think she would make it out of the hospital.

Emily did recover enough to go home from the hospital, but she cried day and night for months from excruciating pain. Maureen got no sleep. Many trips to the doctor and numerous medications made no difference. Her baby continued to cry until she was exhausted. Then she would fall asleep for a while, only to awaken crying again.

At three o'clock one morning Maureen sat shivering on the bathroom floor by the space heater, holding her thirteen-month-old baby. Helpless, exhausted, and burdened, Maureen's tears flowed along with Emily's. "God, I cannot do this anymore," she cried. "I'm turning Emily over to you. I can't figure this out. I can't make any decisions. I'll help her and do whatever you show me."

Maureen's helplessness was God's opportunity to step in, and it was the beginning of healing for both of them. "Nothing happened immediately except the heavy weight began to lessen," Maureen says. "But things did change from that point. I felt God was in charge and *I* was the one helping. Shortly after, the doctors discovered medication that eased Emily's pain. I found myself praying for God's guidance and wisdom for the doctors, and my frantic feelings began to fade."

At eighteen months, the doctors said Emily had only three weeks to live. But she has far surpassed their gloomy predictions. Although disabled and in a wheelchair, seven-year-old Emily improves every day. She's a healthy and happy child who brings her family much joy. And Maureen knows that she's never alone in this, that Jesus meant it when He said, "Come to Me, all you who are weary and burdened, and I will give you rest."

RELEASE BRINGS FREEDOM FOR US AS WELL

"I've totally given my children, especially my oldest, and their problems over to God numerous times—when I should have had to do it only once. I obviously haven't totally given them to Him," one mother confessed.

Can you relate to this mom's dilemma? Do you sometimes even wonder if God gets tired of your bringing your kids to Him in prayer? Fortunately, He knows releasing is tough for parents. He knows because He gave up His son, allowing Him to come to earth, to suffer and die on the cross. He understands our pain in letting go.

Cheryl, the mother of three sons who are twenty-eight, twenty-six, and twenty-four, has learned the wisdom of releasing them daily. She prays, "Lord, I'm not sure what it's going to take to conform them to the image of Christ, but I release them into Your hands for You to conform to Your purposes and plans." She says, "Lord, these are my thoughts and plans, this is the character I'd like to see, but even these I release if it's not the character and plan You have for them. I'm committed to love them and bless them however and whatever you do or they do." She's through wringing her hands, because she realizes that although we want good things for our children, their heavenly Father is looking for their ultimate good. Where we want an immediate fix to the problems, He's making heart changes in our children.

At some time in our children's lives, we must eventually do in the spiritual and emotional realm what Hannah did in the physical realm when she took Samuel to the temple to live: dedicate them and entrust them to God. Otherwise, we smother, cling, and try to control.

Releasing our children isn't easy and it isn't a quick fix; it may come with much struggle and after many tears. It may happen in a watershed moment and then progress as events require more releasing, but each time the releasing becomes more complete until one day our kids truly have their "wings."

While we don't abdicate our responsibilities for nurturing, teaching, or praying for them, this prayer of relinquishment brings us into rest. We do it, accepting that we were never really in control in the first place, that our children aren't really ours but God's, and that we're to care for them but not control them. We do it, knowing that God has a future and a hope for our kids, not calamity (Jeremiah 29:11). As we put our children's hands in His heavenly hands, we gain the freedom to trust God and enjoy our children and life more as we trust Him for direction and help.

PUTTING FEET TO OUR PRAYERS

So how do we learn to pray this most difficult prayer, the prayer of release? Perhaps some of these suggestions will be helpful.

Light a candle. After you've given your child's problem to God, light a candle as a reminder. As you walk through your house, each time you pass by the candle, it can remind you that the problem has been turned over to God and that you can trust His care.

Remember that prayer is for the helpless. When you feel helpless, whether it's from a situation like Maureen faced or from dealing with a rebellious teen or a child with learning problems, don't let it keep you from praying. Your helplessness can actually open a door to hope. As O. Hallesby, the great Norwegian prayer-theologian said, "Prayer is for the helpless."

When our understanding of how little we can do is coupled with our faith in all God can do, we open the door to His power. We then come to Him with a "humble and contrite heart that knows we can't merit anything from God or change the situation ourselves. We just surrender to Him like an infant surrenders to his mother's care."[2] Hallesby uses a wonderful analogy we mothers can easily identify with to explain this secret of effective prayer. "Your infant children cannot formulate in words a single petition to you. Yet the little ones pray the best way they know how. All they can do is cry, but you understand very well their pleading. Moreover, the little ones need not even cry. All you need to do is to see them in all their helpless dependence upon you, and a prayer touches your mother-heart, a prayer which is stronger than the loudest cry."[3]

Just as we hear and respond to an infant, God responds to us. Only He does it perfectly and eternally![4]

Maybe, like me, you breathe a sigh of relief to know that your helplessness doesn't prevent you from coming to God, that in fact it can usher you into His arms. For when we're helpless, we open our hearts and let Him come into our distress or crisis.

Reflect: What do you feel most helpless about in your life or in your children's lives? Bring that very need and your sense of helplessness about it to God today.

Thank You, Lord, that You meet moms in all the crises
and everyday problems of our children's lives and our own lives.
Thank You even for our helplessness because that draws us to You.
I want to trust You and believe that when we call to You, You are there.
Thank You that we don't have to have the problems figured out,
that we can merely bring ourselves and our children to You
and know we are safe in Your hands.

In Your Son's name. Amen.

Oh, that we would turn eye and heart
from everything else
and fix them upon this God who hears prayer
until the magnificence of His promises
and His power and His purpose of love
overwhelmed us!

ANDREW MURRAY

CHAPTER FIVE

Sending Your Child and Prayers to School

"Again I say to you, that if two of you agree
on earth about anything
that they may ask,
it shall be done for them
by My Father who is in heaven."

MATTHEW 18:19

The big day has finally arrived. The first day of first grade.

You've prepared her as best you can. You've bought her new shoes and a new dress. You've armed her with the sixty-four pack of crayons, scissors, glue, and enough No. 2 pencils to last her till puberty. You've packed her Barbie lunch box with healthy food and a little note to reassure her—just in case. But when that car door opens and she walks toward that school looking so grown up and yet so little, you have to let go and place her in someone else's hands.

You wonder, "Will the teacher see the gifts and talents in my child that I do? Will she like my child, and will my little one like her? Will the classroom be a positive environment where she can learn and bloom? Can I trust this teacher to make it a good year for her?"

You've protected your little one and taught her she is a special creature loved by God. But now it's time for her to go to school—a major transition of control. No longer will you be in charge of her day. Other people—teachers, principals—will make decisions that affect her. She'll use materials and books you didn't pick. She may be tempted by peer pressure or hurt by failure, learning problems, or other children.

What can you or any mother do? Though you can't go to school with her, your prayers—in a real and tangible way—can! And through those prayers, God can not only guide and protect your child, but He can impact a whole school and a faculty.

FROM SMALL BEGINNINGS

As Fern Nichols stood in her kitchen one fall morning in 1984, she watched her sons Ty and Troy leave for their first day in junior high in their community of Abbotsford, British Columbia. She knew her boys would be facing new tests in resisting immoral values, vulgar language, and peer pressure. What she'd heard about the use of alcohol and drugs and the high percentage of sexually active teens at the school worried her. Her heart cried out to God, asking Him to protect them and to help them make good decisions.

Fern's mind went back to the previous year when Ty had attended a Christian school on a basketball scholarship. When she was asked to be the devotional chairman for the women's auxiliary group, it had seemed natural to gather the moms to pray weekly for the school and their children. She remembered the support they had all felt and the many answers to prayer they'd seen in the school and their children. It had been a phenomenal time.

"Lord," she said aloud, "it was wonderful praying for the Christian school, but how much more does this junior high need prayer! There must be *one* mom at that junior high who would come and join me."

Immediately a mother's name came to her mind, and when Fern asked if she was interested in praying together, she readily agreed. She too had a burden for her children and welcomed the support of praying with another person. They thought of two or three other moms, and the next week met for prayer.

Fern didn't have to develop materials or a program because the year before she had written a format and guidelines that had worked effectively for the mothers' prayer group:

- They would meet for one hour a week to pray for their children and the school.
- They would start and end on time (important for busy women).
- There would be no dues or refreshments and no social time to talk or gossip about the kids or school problems.
- They would follow the four steps of prayer: praise, confession, thanksgiving, and intercession.
- They would pray "in one accord" conversationally, concentrating on one subject at a time.
- Any number of mothers could pray on each subject until that subject was completely covered.
- Everything that was mentioned in the prayers stayed confidential within the group.

Using this simple format, the mothers met each week and prayed—and saw specific answers to their prayer. The group grew as more mothers wanted to participate. Word spread about how wonderful it was to pray for your kids instead of worrying about them. Before long, moms with children in other schools called Fern, saying, "We need a prayer group for our school. Could you come and tell us what to do?"

God enlarged Fern's heart as she shared her idea of moms praying for schools. She soon found herself invited into many homes to share the format and guidelines for the hour of prayer. In a year's time almost thirty groups started, and other opportunities opened to share with women in churches. Moms In Touch had begun.

Then in the summer of 1985, the Nichols family moved back to the U.S. from British Columbia to Poway, California, where one of Fern's sons entered Poway High School. Fern took the ministry of Moms In Touch with her, gathering a few mothers to pray with her for the school and their children. God met them mightily, and they saw many answers to prayer. Women began calling from all over, asking Fern to help them start a group to pray for their schools, so the ministry of Moms In Touch spread across California, then the United States, and even to other countries.

THE POWER OF UNITED PRAYER

What makes Moms In Touch so appealing and effective? I believe it comes in part from the unique dynamic in united prayer. Matthew 18:19–20 explains one key foundation for the effectiveness of group praying: "Again I say to you, that if two of you agree on earth about anything that they may ask, it shall be done for them by My Father who is in heaven. For where two or three have gathered together in My name, there I am in their midst." What a promise!

While there is power in an individual's prayer, united prayer has even greater power. As author Rosalind Rinker says, "Praying with other people gives us new sisters…in Christ. The more we pray with other people the more we begin to trust them, and the more honest we all can be about our personal needs. Self-consciousness drops away, and we can pray about our real problems, not just surface ones. Genuine togetherness is a God-given state, and hearts are joined in His presence. We can depend upon that presence because He has said, 'I am right there with them.'"[1]

Group praying responds to Paul's admonition for us to "bear one another's burdens." As Rinker says, "Jesus knows that the problems of life press in upon us when we are alone until the spirit is almost broken,"[2] but when those burdens are shared, they become lighter.

I love how Petro, a mother in a Moms In Touch International (MITI) group in Switzerland, put it: "Every Wednesday morning when we gather to pray for our children, it is as if we were weaving our prayers into one another to form a rug under our children—and to strengthen our faith in our Almighty God. What a gift to pray together, making all our praise and anxieties known to Him! And what a gift to have Christian women partners in prayer; when they pray, it is almost as if they adopt my children and commit them to God."

A group of five mothers in Carrollton, Texas, discovered the benefits when they showed up for the very first meeting of McCoy Elementary School MITI and quickly discovered that four of them had a child with learning problems.

"There are two things I'll never forget," says Martha, the leader. "First, the incredible feeling of bearing each other's burdens and how that lessened our anxiety. None of us had ever had someone to pray with us about our child's disabilities. Second was how our mascara ran! We cried and cried together that day and went away feeling that God had given us something we really needed...a sense that we weren't alone."

Another strength of praying in a group is that it brings greater consistency to our prayer life, a concern that many women express. Perhaps our prayer time isn't as regular as we'd like it to be. Maybe we don't feel like we're giving enough attention in prayer to some needs. Then guilt sets in, and we think, "I can't do this. I'll never be a prayer warrior. Why try?" That's just what the enemy wants—to discourage us so we'll give up on daily prayer. But if we're consistently praying each week with other mothers for our children and their schools, for that one hour we're focusing on some of the needs that concern us most. And that consistent time of united prayer will ripple out into our daily, personal prayer life.

SPREADING THE BLANKET OF PRAYER

"One of the most remarkable things about praying with other moms is that you think you know what your child needs—until another mother prays for something you've never thought of. Then a third mom prays for your child's needs from a different angle, and you begin to sense the Spirit covering your child. It's wonderful to feel that!" says Becky, an Oklahoma mother.

When her son Joseph was in the first grade, he was put in a learning disabled (LD) program because he was having difficulty learning to read. The family had to move several times, and by the time he entered third grade in Broken Arrow, Oklahoma, he tested at a first-grade reading level and was struggling in school. Becky hated seeing him discouraged day after day. She was discouraged herself, and worried, and all alone in their new location.

Then Becky heard about the mothers' prayer group at the school and began to attend weekly. The other mothers joined her in praying for Joseph not only once a week, but every day in their own devotional times.

When diagnostic testing was being done, the group prayed earnestly for Joseph. They asked God to provide wisdom for those testing him and to guard them from stereotyping or wrongfully labeling him. They prayed for God's help in every aspect of Joseph's learning and for his confidence to grow. They wept with Becky when things were hard and rejoiced when Joseph's schoolwork began to improve.

After months of prayer, God's answer could be seen. When Joseph was tested again in May, he'd made remarkable progress, going from a first-grade reading level to a fourth-grade level. "When school started this fall, the teachers and principal said he had done so well they were assigning him to regular classes instead of the LD class," says Becky. "It meant so much to know that I wasn't alone, that even when I was at home praying for Joseph, other moms were praying too!"

PRAYING FOR THE TEACHERS

While it's easy to pray for our children's needs, it's harder to pray for those who direct their days, especially if we disapprove of them or their teaching style. But how much more important it is to lift them up to God when we question their positive influence on our children.

In the early grades when children are in a self-contained classroom and spend their entire day with one teacher, many moms pray for getting "just the right teacher"—the one who will bring out the best in their children. Parents will go to great lengths to ensure a good match. But what do you do when your child has just been assigned the worst teacher in the school? Can your prayers make a difference for the teacher and your child?

B.J. experienced this on Orientation Day. She and her second grader, Austin, were looking up and down the class rosters taped to the wall to find his assigned teacher. As B.J. located Austin's name, tears began to trickle down her face.

"Mom, are those tears of joy?" Austin asked.

"Yes, she's the teacher God chose for you," his mom replied with a hug.

Actually, B.J. was crying because her son had been assigned the harshest, most critical teacher in the school.

Sure enough, the teacher quickly developed a particular dislike for Austin. Right in front of other students and parents, she would blurt out to B.J., "Your child was horrible today! You need to..." She put him down regularly in class. Austin responded to her actions by giving her trouble. Conflict and problems escalated.

But B.J. was committed to not being critical around Austin. Instead, she volunteered in the school and saw firsthand the teacher's frustrations with her class. B.J. looked for things she did well to compliment, both to the teacher and to Austin. She encouraged him to cooperate with his teacher.

Most of all, she prayed for this teacher every single week at Moms In Touch. She was led to pray Acts 26:18, asking God to open the teacher's eyes and turn her from darkness to light so she could receive forgiveness of sins and a place among those who are saved by faith in Christ. Things didn't improve for Austin in the classroom, but as the months went by and they continued praying, B.J. sensed he was in this teacher's class for a purpose.

In May, the teacher attended a revival at a church in their city, and there she accepted Christ. During the last weeks of school, the moms saw an amazing transformation in her life. Encouragement replaced harshness and criticism.

Now, years later, B.J. hears from that MITI group how wonderful and loving this teacher is; she's become a favorite with the kids and parents. Now when she comes over to the middle school for meetings, she seeks out Austin just to say hello. Or if she sees B.J., she asks, "How's your son?"

"Our group prays change, not removal, if teachers are difficult," says B.J. "After all, they might be moved to a school that doesn't have a MITI group! We pray that God will soften their hearts, and it's amazing how many teachers we've seen be touched by Him."

Another success story is the young art teacher at the school, whose classroom was truly out of control. He would literally pull his hair, ranting and raving at his students. For a full year the MITI group lifted him up every week during intercession time. The next year God softened his heart toward the children by giving him and his wife their first baby. This teacher has grown to be one of the kids' favorites and was recently named "Teacher of the Year."

PRAYING FOR ISSUES

Because the weapons we wield in prayer are spiritual weapons, we don't have to go to the principal or the board to fight all the battles. As 2 Corinthians 10:4 says, "The weapons we fight with are not the weapons of the world. On the contrary, they have divine power to demolish strongholds" (NIV). We may accomplish more on our knees than on our soapboxes. And that doesn't apply just to the big issues like sex education, textbooks, and curriculum; prayer also can affect the practical decisions. (Yes, once again, God reminds us He's willing to work in the ordinary details as well as the grand schemes.)

In one school, for example, carpet was going to be installed during the two weeks before Christmas break, forcing the teachers to hold classes in the hallways (as if those weeks aren't chaotic enough already!). The mothers prayed that the carpet wouldn't arrive until Christmas break so it wouldn't disrupt learning. Despite the principal telling the teachers every day, "Prepare to move your desks into the halls because the carpet will be here tomorrow," the carpet didn't show up until the day after the students left for Christmas.

In an Illinois school, the moms group had been praying since school started that the principal, even though he was not a Christian, would downplay the satanic aspect of Halloween and make the school celebrations more wholesome. None of the mothers talked to him about their concerns, but, instead, battled on their knees and trusted God to do His part. Two weeks before Halloween, the principal announced that he was concerned about the dark side of the holiday. He had decided the class parties would have a circus theme and that no witch or vampire costumes would be allowed.

At other times, however, mothers' prayer groups do play a visible role in the decision making. At the beginning of the 1996 school year, the Canby, Oregon, district was plagued by problems and a pending strike by the teachers' union. When the Moms In Touch groups hosted a back-to-school breakfast for the area pastors and school administrators, the superintendent asked the mothers to pray for the teacher contract negotiations that were to begin in October.

The moms prayed every week for both the teachers and the school administrators. They prayed for unity so that the new contracts might be agreeable to both teachers and administrators. They prayed for the Christian teachers to see their job as a ministry and for God to provide for them. Most of all they prayed that the decision makers' vision would be what was best for the children. Their prayers were answered mightily when both sides accepted the new contracts and a strike was avoided.

Nanci, a MITI group leader in Hawaii, knows the difference mothers' prayers make. Last fall she saw a small article on the back page of the newspaper, announcing that condoms would be distributed that week in an elementary and a high school in a sparsely populated area of Kauai. Concerned about how that would affect the children, Nanci called her group of moms to intercede. The mothers prayed earnestly for the children around the clock. By that Thursday night, the front-page article in the newspaper read, "No condoms will be allowed in Hawaii schools."

"I've learned through many years of praying for our kids and their schools, it's prayer that changes things," says Nanci.

PRAYING FOR PRINCIPALS

Perhaps more than any other person, a principal influences a school's learning environment and atmosphere. Even if the principal doesn't believe in prayer, he can hardly withstand the power that is called down upon him by a group of earnest and sincere moms praying in concert.

A principal in Lewisville, Texas, was diagnosed with brain cancer at the beginning of the school year, which meant surgery, then radiation therapy, and months off the job. The doctors' prognosis for recovery was extremely negative. The principal's philosophy was "God is out there somewhere but doesn't have much to do with me." (Little did he know.) The moms group prayed every week during the school year for his healing and strength, but especially that the experience would draw him closer to God.

By spring as the principal gradually regained strength, he began coming back to school part-time. After his brain scans in May and July indicated he was completely clear of cancer, he was able to return full-time the next fall.

"The most exciting thing, however, was the change we saw in him," says Nicki, the MITI leader. On Orientation Day a parent asked how he was feeling, to which he replied, "I praise God every day for my health!" In the school newsletters he has continued to express gratitude for all those who prayed for him and for the miracle of good health.

Even when circumstances aren't so life-threatening, praying moms can impact principals through their constant prayer support. Barbara, the

MITI group leader for Rollings Hills, a San Diego elementary school, approached their principal to let him know they would be praying for him and the school. Although he was willing for the moms to give the teachers and staff the treats they had prepared, he was uncomfortable with the prayers.

Within a year, this principal was transferred to a different school in the area. As he served there for seven years, he was surrounded by Christian teachers and parents and a Moms In Touch group that continued the prayers for his salvation. When he was later transferred to a third school, another MITI group continued the vigil, praying for him for two more years.

After ten years of constant and countless prayers from three different Moms In Touch groups, this principal accepted Christ at a local church. He's now a strong witness for Christ among the other principals and administrators in the San Diego and Poway districts.

When your child starts school…

When you're concerned about a teacher, a principal, a textbook, a curriculum…

When you worry about the barrage of new influences on that little one you have nurtured…

Pray!

Then find another mom or a group of moms who will pray with you.

God will meet you there.

PUTTING FEET TO OUR PRAYERS

Here are some practical ways to put these ideas to work.

Gather two or three in His Name. It doesn't take a gymnasium full of people for God to move in your school. Ask God to provide one other mom to join you each week in prayer. Once you find that mother and begin meeting, pray that God will bring other moms who want to intercede for their children. In the meantime, start praying about a problem the school has or a teacher who is having a difficult time. If you want to start your own Moms In Touch group, call 1-800-949-MOMS or write MITI; P.O. Box 1120; Poway, CA 92074-1120, and ask for a booklet and leader's guidelines; they'll provide everything you need to get started. They can also direct you to someone who can tell you if a Moms In Touch group already exists in your area that you could join.

Find a prayer partner. Some problems can't wait a week to be prayed over. What a blessing to have someone you can call at a moment's notice to pray. Two moms I know trade prayer lists for their children's needs each week and then pray at least once a week on the phone.

Peggy—my prayer partner—and I pray frequently on the phone for our combined lot of eight children (five of them in college!). Knowing she will take the request right to the Lord in prayer and keep it confidential means the world to me.

Use the Four Steps of Prayer. For group prayers as well as private prayers, try the classic method of praying that Moms In Touch groups use: Praise, Confession, Thanksgiving, and Intercession. So often we lay our children's needs before God like a laundry list and forget to thank Him for the way He answered last week's prayers. The four steps of prayer can focus our thoughts and keep them from straying.

- *Praise*—First spend a few moments in praise, focusing on God's character and attributes instead of on the problems. Concentrating on our God's omnipotence frees us from our burdens, and our praise draws us nearer to Him. "Praise lifts our eyes from the battle to the victor. Praise drives away frustration, tension, depression, and fear. Praise cleanses the atmosphere, gets rid of all the smog and fog so that we can see clearly who is in control. Our focus is drawn from the complexity of the problem to the adequacy of God's infinite resources,"[3] says Fern Nichols.

  The Bible, especially Psalms, is full of praise passages and snapshots of God's character which can inspire our praise. Read a psalm aloud to God to praise Him. If you're really down in the dumps, pray the last seven psalms back to God, one each day for a week; your heart will overflow with praise. God loves to hear us say we love Him!

- *Confession* —Confession is agreeing with God that we have sinned, and it restores us to fellowship with Him. It's an important part of any prayer time, because the truth is, if we hold on to wickedness in our heart, the Lord will not hear our prayers (Isaiah 59:2). Ask God to shine His light and show you any words, actions, or attitudes not pleasing to Him, any grudge or quarrel that's unresolved. When you speak honestly with God about your sins and where you fall short, you can depend on God to cleanse you (1 John 1:9). Then ask God to fill you with His Spirit and direct your petitions.
- *Thanksgiving*—Thank and honor God for what He has done. (See 1 Thessalonians 5:18 and Psalm 50:23.) Ask Him to help you remember the answers to prayers He has provided. Often we ask God to do so many things that we fail to notice when the answers come! We can thank Him for material, physical, and spiritual blessings, for the gift of our children, and most of all, for salvation through Christ.
- *Intercession*—Intercession means entreaty in favor of another, standing in the gap for others. Intercession time is love on our knees, when we aren't praying for our own needs but for others—our children, their classmates, teachers, and school community.

Our prayers can be simple and short, like Peter's "Lord, save me," or like the contrite man's "God be merciful to me, a sinner." It is not the composition of the words but of the heart behind them that matters. And when we base our requests on God's Word by praying specific scriptures, He fills us with confidence, because we know we are asking in harmony with His will.

Lord, make me a faithful intercessor for my children.
Show me what's on Your heart for them
that I might pray in harmony with Your will for their lives.
Widen my heart to pray for their teachers and their school,
and bring other moms to join me in prayer.
Thank You that as I pray, the Holy Spirit intercedes,
that I don't have to have the answers or solutions
because You do!

In Jesus' name. Amen.

Our prayers lay the track down
on which God's power can come.
Like a mighty locomotive,
his power is irresistible,
but it cannot reach us without rails.

WATCHMAN NEE

CHAPTER SIX

THE PERSISTENCE OF A LONG-RANGE PRAYER

At all times they ought
to pray and not to lose heart.
LUKE 18:1

You've never experienced winter until you've experienced it in Maine. We were snowbound. It was nine degrees below zero. And it was Sunday.

Thinking it unwise to brave the roads to church, we decided to have family worship time at home. After Holmes opened in prayer and read the Bible aloud, I gave each of our three children a blank sheet of white paper and asked them to draw a picture, depicting our relationship with God and how we felt about Him. Being an educator at heart, I thought it would stimulate a good spiritual discussion.

After a few moments of pondering and sketching, they shared their pictures. Alison, age eleven, showed us a big heart with a little girl inside. "That's me, right close to God's heart," she explained.

Chris, thirteen, held out his detailed picture of a brick window ledge and a boy just barely hanging on to the windowsill. "That's how I feel right now with all the changes and a new school—I'm hanging on to God," he said.

When it was Justin's turn to share, our fifteen-year-old son held up a blank sheet of paper and announced he had things to do in his room upstairs.

My heart sank.

LORD, TEACH ME TO PRAY

When Justin had started high school, his heart began to wander from God, and he quickly left his childlike faith behind. Being accepted, being part of the popular, party group at school was a higher priority than being with the youth group. Granted, he had gone through some tough experiences. He'd been disillusioned with a youth minister. He was disappointed with God when his dad's business faltered, causing us to move two thousand miles from friends. And his best friend back home had been critically injured in a car wreck. With each tragedy, he put more distance between himself and God.

My concern about our son was matched only by my feelings of helplessness to change his heart or the situation, but that very helplessness lit a fire under me. I devoted more time to investigating how I might pray for him more effectively. "Lord, teach me to pray for my children," I asked. "Make me a faithful intercessor! Show me their needs, give me Your perspective, and help me to cooperate with Your will for their lives" became my continual prayer.

God was just waiting for me to ask. I began to find such clear directions in the Bible on how to intercede effectively. Sometime before in my daily devotions I had started praying scriptures back to God. Occasionally, when a passage spoke to my need or one of our children's needs, I would write the name and the date in the margin of my Bible to remind me to continue praying that verse. For instance, when I read Colossians 2:6–7, I wrote "Prayer for J, C, and A" in the margin. I prayed that since they had received Christ Jesus the Lord, they would have the grace to "walk in Him, having been firmly rooted and now being built up in Him and established in [their] faith...and overflowing with gratitude."

So now I asked the Spirit to show me His will—and the specific verses to pray for our son. He led me to Ephesians, so I prayed each day "that the God of our Lord Jesus Christ, the glorious Father, would give [him] the Spirit of wisdom and revelation," so that he would know the Father better. I prayed "that the eyes of [his] heart may be enlightened" (to have the light bulb of spiritual understanding come on) so that he would "know the hope" he'd been called to in Christ, the great purpose and plan God had for his life (1:17–18, NIV). When he had a decision to make, I prayed he would be filled with the knowledge of God's will "in all spiritual wisdom and understanding" so he could walk in a way that pleased God (Colossians 1:9–10).

I didn't know how God was going to accomplish these feats. In fact, many times I didn't feel like anything was happening. The situation surely wasn't changing as far as I could see. However, the more I prayed for our son, the less I worried about him. Whether Justin was changing or not, praying these Scriptures strengthened my own faith because I knew I was asking in line with God's will, as stated right there in the Bible.

I knew those verses reflected what God wanted for our son—a close relationship with Him, a purpose, a hope—and I realized God through His Spirit yearned over Justin and desired that he come home to Christ even more than I did! After all, He had been the very one to put the verses in my heart to pray for Justin.

So my confidence in God and in His promises grew as I continued to pray day after day, week after week, month after month—yet outwardly, still nothing changed. After graduation, Justin went to a college out of state and eight hours away. Although I continued to pray the Word over his life, I could really feel our influence slipping away.

PRAY GOD'S WORD

Why pray Scripture? As I talk with women, one of their frustrations with prayer is not knowing what to say to God or how to express it. "It sounds better to me when someone else prays," said one woman. "I don't feel my words are right."

Without His Word, I find our prayers become dry, lifeless, and vague. With His Word, our prayers are nourished and what we need to pray is illumined. "True prayer is God's words in your mouth," says Jennifer Dean in *The Praying Life*. God's words are alive and active, sharper than a two-edged sword, Hebrews 4:12 tells us. God promises that His Word will bear fruit: "So is my word that goes out from my mouth: It will not return to me empty, but will accomplish what I desire and achieve the purpose for which I sent it" (Isaiah 55:11, NIV).

My friend Melanie has seen how praying God's Word can accomplish His purpose. Several years ago she was deeply concerned about her sister Karen. She wasn't walking with Christ, and her two teenagers had run away from home in rebellion, refusing even to speak to their grandparents or Melanie. Melanie knew other family members had tried to talk to Karen, but talking had no effect.

So Melanie set aside special pages in her prayer journal. On the left side, she wrote down what she was praying for: her sister's salvation, her niece's and nephew's return home and to Christ, the relationships. In the middle of the page, she wrote out the verses she was going to pray for her sister. And on the right side of the page at the top she wrote "Date Fulfilled."

Every day instead of moaning to God about the awful situation, Melanie prayed those verses. Even though she heard discouraging news about the niece and nephew, she kept praying God's Word. And as she did, God strengthened her faith that He was going to do the impossible.

Within a year, Karen was saved, and relationships had been restored. The wayward teens had miles to go in maturity, but they were back on a positive track.

"The more we incorporate the Scriptures into our praying, the more likely we are to pray in the will of God, for God always stands behind what

He has said," says Judson Cornwall.[1] Psalm 138:2–3 confirm it: "For your promises are backed by all the honor of your name. When I pray, you answer me, and encourage me by giving me the strength I need" (TLB).

Catherine Marshall, wife of Peter Marshall, explained what she found written in her husband's Bible: "It's the word of a Gentleman of the most sacred and strictest honour, and there's an end on it! —David Livingstone"

Below it was Peter's signature. When she asked about the statement, he explained: "In these pages are the living words of the living God. These words include a lot of promises, many of them with conditions attached. All we have to do is to meet the conditions, then step up and claim them."

When we pray those promises for our children or ourselves—verses like Jeremiah 29:11 ("'I know the plans I have for you,' declares the LORD, 'plans to prosper you and not to harm you, plans to give you hope and a future,'" NIV) and Philippians 4:19 ("God shall supply all your needs according to His riches in glory in Christ Jesus")—our prayers become filled with faith instead of doubt. We trust God to fulfill the promises in His way and on His timetable.

BE PATIENT AND PERSISTENT

In this long adventure of praying for Justin (at least it felt long to me), I continued writing down God's promises and verses as He seemed to point them out as applying to Justin's situation. Still nothing changed on the outside. He pledged a fraternity in college, partied with the guys all weekend, slept in on Sunday mornings, and dodged any serious discussions when home for a holiday. Spiritual talk was out of the question. He seemed more distant from God than ever. "It's my faith, Mom. I can't go on what you and Dad believe," he said one day when I probed. "I've got to figure things out, and I'm not sure what I believe now."

"Persevere in prayer, and trust me," God seemed to say when my spirits flagged. One way He encouraged me was through the stories of mothers in history who had prayed for their kids who were "in the far country." Reading them, I was reminded my situation wasn't new; God's been in the business of drawing prodigals home for a long time. These mothers of earlier centuries felt the same concerns I did. They grieved when their sons and daughters strayed from the faith, and they wanted them to yield their lives to Christ instead of to the world.

One of my favorite stories was of Monica, the mother of Augustine, who eventually became one of the great fathers of the Christian church. But you would never have predicted it when he was a teenager! The rebellious young Augustine lived with a mistress at sixteen, fathered an illegitimate son, and eventually joined a cult. (This mother's struggles put mine in the shade.)

Augustine wouldn't even listen to his mother talk about her Christian faith or beliefs, so she prayed more fervently. As an adolescent, he reveled in the company of fellow sinners, later describing it as wallowing "in slime, striving often to rise, but being all the more heavily dashed down."[2] The battle between Augustine's flesh and his spirit was a fierce one that lasted years. In fact, Monica prayed for her wayward son for over nineteen years before her prayers prevailed.

After his conversion, Augustine described the impact of his mother's prayers by saying, "And now didst thou stretch forth thy hand from above and didst draw my soul up out of that profound darkness because my mother, thy faithful one, wept to thee on my behalf more than mothers are accustomed to weep for the bodily deaths of their children."[3] That's powerful and persistent prayer.

Through these stories of other mothers, I also became aware that those who have a great spiritual calling often face a great attack on their lives in their youth. Do you know the story of Hudson Taylor, founder of the China Inland Mission? Although his parents dedicated him to God for mission work in China even before he was born and raised him in a godly home, he went through troubled times as a teenager. He rebelled against his father and experienced many spiritual doubts, leading his mother and sister to pray constantly for him.

When Taylor was seventeen and in great turmoil, his mom was so concerned for his soul that she locked herself in a room at her sister's house fifty miles away, resolving to stay there in prayer until she had clear assurance from God that He'd heard and answered her prayers for Hudson's conversion. Taylor later reported that the exact afternoon she interceded so dramatically for him he read "a gospel tract about the finished work of Christ and accepted this Savior and this salvation."[4]

Several months later during an intense prayer for guidance, Taylor heard God calling him to China, and immediately he began preparing and studying for the mission field. As a result of his life's work, millions of Chinese heard the gospel of Christ, and a whole generation of missionaries was inspired.

DON'T GIVE UP

Armed with this inspiration of praying mothers and transformed sons, I continued my prayer campaign for our son. After Justin's freshman year, he decided to transfer to the University of Oklahoma, an hour away from home. Maybe he *had* changed, I hoped. Perhaps he would go to church with us or connect with the college youth group.

My hopes died when, after being home only a few days, he started dating "The Girlfriend from the Pit," ushering us into one of our most difficult summers on record. This girl was headed down a path of destruction and quickly began dragging him with her.

Praying alone day after day over the same issues, I had become battle weary and felt the need for the support of other women. I had prayed in a few other groups through the years but work pressures had caused me to become a solitary intercessor. So after a few months of nudging from God, in the fall I started a Moms In Touch group for Chris and Alison's high school.

As the months of that school year passed, I was encouraged by how God was answering prayers in our teens' lives—if not visibly in our older son's life. I was touched each week as I watched moms lift their children up to God together. The burden felt less crushing, the problem not so impossible. With renewed confidence in God, women left prayer time, heads held high, feeling less stress and more joy, because they knew their kids were in God's hands.

BE READY FOR A SURPRISE

All that year I continued to pray for Alison, Chris, and Justin, now a sophomore in college. Although he was closer to home, he was no closer to God. I knew his roommate had no relationship with Christ, so the Lord enlarged my heart further, and I began to intercede for him also.

The months went by. A girlfriend or two passed through his life. Weeks of busy classes and activities filled his time, but no spiritual change—not until Justin moved back home to scour the city for a summer job.

Following dinner one night, he asked me to drive him across town to pick up his overheated car stuck on the side of a highway. Never one to pass up an opportunity to talk one-on-one with my children—even as a taxi driver—I went.

On the way to get the car towed, Justin talked about all kinds of things. He shared his frustrations about trying to find a summer job and his disappointment about a dating relationship that had gone sour. Then he turned to me and said, "You know, Mom, I'm feeling awfully empty and lonely, being so far from God and trying to do everything on my own. I know that God hasn't moved; I have. But what I want more than anything is to have an intimate relationship with Christ. I want to really know Him."

He never looked back. As his heart returned to God, God faithfully met him right where he was and took him along a path of growth. Only a few days later he had the opportunity to attend Summit Ministries camp in Colorado, where he was offered a job on staff for the whole summer, working maintenance and leading small groups of high school boys. He grew a lot that summer, but when he returned for his junior year at OU, I was concerned he had no Christian friends or support for his faith there.

"Turn your concern into prayer," I seemed to be hearing. So I prayed all summer for a group that would continue to disciple him and help him grow. After being back at college a week, he was invited to a Young Life leadership retreat where he met many other believers. He found a men's Bible study on campus with graduate and law students who were a little farther along in their walk with God. He also had the opportunity to attend several dynamic Christian conferences that year. He grew by leaps and bounds, and God did immeasurably more than all I'd asked or imagined.

As our son's heart changed, his music, priorities, and habits changed. His view of girls changed. "I can't imagine dating a girl who isn't sold out to Christ," he told us one night after the three of us had been to a movie. (In high school we never could convince him of the wisdom of dating Christian girls.)

Justin's heart turned back to the family. He asked how he could pray for us. He wanted to spend more time with us. He even wanted to spend more time with his younger brother and sister (who almost fainted at this newfound interest in them). As he led a Bible study for high school boys, his talents in teaching and communication began to bloom.

During that year he fell in love with a beautiful Christian girl named Tiffany, for which I rejoiced. They married in May 1994 and serve the Lord together by leading a college house church and serving in our church's student ministry. Justin speaks at youth services, where his special compassion and understanding of the situations and temptations that young men struggle with give him a ready audience.

However, don't think we've "arrived" spiritually at our house. I have a twenty-year-old and twenty-two-year-old for whom I'm in constant prayer. And many days *I* need encouragement to keep going and not get discouraged.

But if the mother of Augustine could pray for more than nineteen years, I suppose I can keep going a bit longer myself.

PUTTING FEET TO OUR PRAYERS

Whether you are just beginning to pray for your children or are discouraged from months or even years of praying without seeing results, consider some of the following suggestions to let God work in your prayers in a fresh way.

Find God's will for your children. The Bible contains promises concerning His plans for your children, the provision He has available, and what He has in store for them both in this life and in the life to come. Look throughout Scripture to see what God desires for young men and women, and let this shape your prayers. For example—

- how He wants them to be "taught of the Lord" and how great will be their (and our) peace! (Isaiah 54:13)
- how He wants them to hide His Word in their hearts, so they won't sin against Him (Psalm 119:11)
- how He wants to fill them with the knowledge of His will (Colossians 1:9)
- how He desires that they not lean on their own understanding but trust Him in all their ways (Proverbs 3:5–6)

If you're having difficulty finding appropriate passages, ask God to show you a verse to pray for your child's specific problem.

Or, look at the prayers in the Bible. From David's confessions and prayers for help to Hannah's prayer of thanksgiving to Jesus' prayers to His Father, biblical prayers can be our patterns. Paul's prayers for his spiritual children can be wonderful guides for praying for your children. Look at Galatians 5:22–23; Ephesians 1:17–19; 3:16–19; Colossians 1:9–10; and 2 Timothy 1:7.

When a verse strikes you as addressing what your child needs, write it down, put his or her initials by it, and date it in your Bible. You might also want to write it on a card as a reminder. Then continue to pray that verse and wait for the fulfillment of God's promise in His timing.

Express gratefulness for the "cloud of witnesses" and intercessors. When I reflect on how our son's life turned around, it reminds me that although my prayers were vital, God also heard the prayers of my mother for him since his infancy, as well as his grandmother Joan's prayers. God was also answering Flo's prayers, my eighty-year-old friend and intercessor who for twenty years has "adopted" me and my children into her circle of daily prayers—and the prayers of my friends Cynthia, Corrie, and Peggy. This fills me with gratefulness!

Who has prayed for you or your children that you could thank? Write them a note today.

Thou hast given so much to me,
Give one thing more—a grateful heart;
Not thankful when it pleaseth me,
As if Thy blessings had spare days,
but such a heart whose pulse may be Thy praise.
GEORGE HERBERT

There is no gift like prayer,
for in prayer we find
a Father who welcomes us,
who listens and always understands,
peace in the perspective of eternity...
strength to hold on and wait for God to work,
a haven in His presence,
a safe place to keep those we love.

UNKNOWN

CHAPTER SEVEN

THE TUG-OF-WAR YEARS:

PRAYING FOR OUR TEENAGERS

Yet those who wait for the LORD
Will gain new strength;
They will mount up with wings like eagles,
They will run and not get tired,
They will walk and not become weary.

ISAIAH 40:31

"What's it like to raise a teenager?" someone asked.

"Do you remember what your child was like in the terrible twos? Just multiply by eight and add a driver's license," the wise mom replied.

Oh, the teenage years. Ever heard yourself say—

"A boy has asked you out on a date?"

"You're going where? With who? Till when?"

"And how much is that going to cost me?"

"That's what you're wearing?"

"What happened to the car?"

"You've never heard of Peter, Paul, and Mary?"

The teen years come with their own unique set of issues. Now our kids are driving their own cars and spending more time with friends, away from family. They're testing their wings—and occasionally taking a nosedive. They're separating from us and developing independence, a natural and necessary process but nonetheless painful.

So what's unique about praying for teenagers? One mom of two teenage daughters summed it up well: "With small children, I had smaller worries and prayers. With teenagers, I have bigger worries—and bigger prayers!"

Face it, at times you probably feel like you're in a tug-of-war. You're pulling your teen toward curfews, homework, family, going to church. And your teen is straining toward fewer and farther boundaries, their own friends, their own decisions. This season of parenting requires more—more energy, more letting go, more trust in God, more trust in prayer—because it's tough to maintain the proper balance among what is our part, our child's part, and God's part in these delicate years.

HELPING THEM FIND THEIR OWN WAY

David started ninth grade at the large, overcrowded high school in the community after two years of being home schooled. Although he was eager to join his classmates, his mom was worried. One of more than five hundred freshmen, David had a full slate of classes, each with a different teacher in a different room and building on the sprawling campus. He wanted so much to fit in that he hesitated to tell teachers about his hearing disability. When he did mention it, he got little help.

Because of severe ear infections and high fevers as a baby, David had a hearing discrimination problem. He could decipher only about 5–8 percent of what was said in certain sound ranges, which made academic work a huge struggle. Despite his best efforts and hours spent studying after school, by midterm he was failing most of his courses.

David determined to try harder but resisted seeking help from his mother, Elaine. Throughout elementary school she had spent hours every day reteaching what he didn't understand in class. Through the middle school grades, she had home schooled him. Even though he was struggling now, he didn't want her pushing or helping him. Truth was, in David's mind, his mother was like a wheelchair—something he appreciated and relied on to get along in school, yet a source of anger also, because it reminded him he wasn't making it on his own.

When David was younger, Elaine could manage both her tasks and his. But as he grew older, the weight of responsibility increased until she was exhausted and almost to the breaking point. Her husband wisely stepped in, realizing he needed to take a greater role in parenting their son and handling school issues.

David continued to study and work hard until his reserves were also depleted, and yet he was still failing. One afternoon after another day of struggling at school, he broke down. "I don't know why God made me; I can't do anything good."

It broke Elaine's heart. Realizing that only God could help, she turned to a Moms In Touch prayer group in her area.

TRUSTING THE KING

Elaine felt like a Moses. In a battle with the fierce Amalekites, the Israelites under Joshua's command had prevailed in battle—as long as Moses held up his hands. But as the battle raged on, Moses became so weary he couldn't stand up or raise his hands any longer. As his hands drooped to his sides, the Amalekites grew stronger and more victorious. Then Moses' friends Aaron and Hur came alongside him and held up his hands. As they supported his arms, Israel prevailed once again, and the battle was won. Elaine, too, needed others to hold her up in the weariness of the battle for her son.

The more she prayed with the group, the more her perspective changed. She was especially impacted by the praise time. "Praise reminded me of who I am talking to and what He has the power to do. Praise lifted my eyes off myself and my worldly vision and allowed me to have a glimpse of the King."

The more she watched her King, the more her fears for David melted away. She realized the King had sent His Son to die for her David, that He had an exciting plan for him, and that the King had all the power and connections to bring His plan for her son to pass. The King reminded her, "Elaine, David is My David. Just as you released him to his earthly father, you need to release him to Me."

As she changed on the inside, Elaine's husband noticed a change on the outside. In response, he began investing hours in praying, studying classic books on prayer, calling other men to pray, and developing a heart for world missions.

David was also impacted by the change in his mom as she began passing on a legacy of faith instead of fear about his future. When he put out his maximum effort and yet failed chemistry, she responded, "Don't worry about it. God has given you everything you need to have a wonderful, exciting career."

David already had a deep faith in God, but now he began to believe in her hope for his future. He prayed and read God's Word every day. He claimed the promise of Proverbs 22:29: "Do you see a man skilled in his work? He will serve before kings" (NIV). He changed from all college-bound electives to some courses he had real interest in, like computers. Although he still struggled in school, his faith and hope grew.

During his four years of high school, Elaine and the group of mothers interceded for David's teachers, his choice of classes, and his ability to understand and pass his courses. When he had trouble, they praised God for directing his path into something else of God's choosing. They prayed for open doors and thanked God for closed ones. The year he graduated from high school, they all celebrated together, for Elaine's friends had grown to love David.

God opened a door to a part-time computer job and to computer animation classes at a local junior college. David was asked to serve on a special team to produce a college catalogue on CD-ROM for incoming students. The project won an award. The next year, David was asked by the college to lead the CD-ROM project and to teach two college seminars on computer animation. Professors began to refer students to David for tutoring.

This year several major ministries called David to discuss CD-ROM possibilities. Then came the most unbelievable call of all. After seeing David's CD-ROM college catalogue, an outstanding Christian university offered him a full scholarship with room, board, and tuition if he would come and produce one for them.

Elaine couldn't wait until the next prayer meeting. It was a time of tears, praise, and genuine rejoicing. With the support of her own "Aarons" and "Hurs," and with God's answers to their prayers, Elaine has helped launch David to be "a man skilled in his work," serving the King of kings!

WEARY IN THE WAITING ROOM

The resolution to David's struggles didn't occur overnight. It took six years of waiting and praying, like much of the work God does in our lives and our children's lives.

But waiting is not a modern virtue. We prefer fast food, express lanes, speed dial, fast forward, quick fixes, and instant potatoes (well, maybe not). Waiting goes against the modern grain. And it is one of the distinctive frustrations of the season of parenting and praying for teenagers.

"Praying for a teen requires a great deal of patience," Brenda confessed. "To wait on the Lord to bring my child through these times is my biggest challenge."

"My greatest frustration is praying for my teen to have spiritual maturity and wondering if I'll live to see it!" said Jean.

"During this season I'm impatient waiting for God to respond," said another mother. "I believe it's because my teenage son is moving too fast." She's exactly right. Sometimes it seems our kids are running at warp speed while God is walking in slow motion.

God must have known this was going to be a challenge, because throughout the Bible He encourages His people to wait, and He assures us of the benefits:

- "Wait for the LORD; be strong, and let your heart take courage; yes, wait for the LORD" (Psalm 27:14).
- "Wait for the LORD, and keep His way, and He will exalt you to inherit the land" (Psalm 37:34).
- "The LORD is good to those who wait for Him" (Lamentations 3:25).

But my favorite promise comes from Isaiah 40: "Those who wait for the LORD will gain new strength; they will mount up with wings like eagles, they will run and not get tired, they will walk and not become weary" (Isaiah 40:31).

God's fulfillment of His promises for our children's lives may depend on our patiently waiting on Him instead of giving up and grumbling. So how can we wait with patience and hope?

First, it helps to see that our waiting is not in vain. "Waiting seems to be a kind of acted-out prayer," said Catherine Marshall. Waiting develops "patience, persistence, trust, expectancy—all the qualities we are continually beseeching God to give us."[1] During our seasons of waiting, she says, "We were learning the great secret of abiding. Abiding is the key to unlock heaven's treasures."[2]

Marshall explains, "God does have His 'fulness' for the answer to each prayer. It follows then that He alone knows the magnitude of the changes that have to be wrought in us before we can receive our hearts' desires. He alone knows the changes and interplay of external events that must take place before our prayer can be answered. That's why Jesus told us, 'It is not for you to know the times or the seasons, which the Father hath put in his own power.'"[3]

There are two things that particularly help me when I get weary in the waiting process. The first is to focus again on the character of God.

KNOW THE CHARACTER OF GOD

The Bible shows how God deals with His people, especially those like Noah, Moses, Abraham, Joseph, David, Daniel, and Hannah who had to wait. How many days of rain did Noah chalk up before he saw a rainbow? How many dusty steps did Moses take before he looked into the promised land? How many stars did Abraham count before he held his promised son? Their lives testify to God's faithfulness.

The "Hall of Faith" in Hebrews 11 is lined with people who did amazing things—they "performed acts of righteousness, obtained promises, shut the mouths of lions, quenched the power of fire, escaped the edge of the sword, from weakness were made strong, became mighty in war.... Women received back their dead by resurrection" (11:33–35). Yet "none of them received all that God had promised them; for God wanted them *to wait* and share the even better rewards that were prepared for us" (11:39–40, TLB, emphasis mine). God works in the lives of those who trust Him and wait for Him to act.

When I get weary of waiting for God to move in the lives of my children, I not only study how he has moved in others' lives, but I look again at the very nature of God by meditating on His names.

He is Jehovah-jireh, Lord, the Provider[4]; just as He provided yesterday, He'll provide in the future. And He'll provide what our teenagers need to be drawn to Him.

He is Jehovah-rapha, Lord, the Healer[5]; He specializes in healing relationships. He can heal our broken hearts and renew our weary spirits.

God is Jehovah-nissi, Lord, the banner[6]—and His banner over us and our teenagers is His love. Picture that banner written across your family and your kids, wherever they are.

He's also Emmanuel, God with us—not at a distance, but whispering in our ear, giving us the wisdom we need. And He is constantly working in our kids' lives, even when we can't see it.

He is Jehovah-shammah, the Lord is there.[7] There is no place our children can go to escape His presence. As Psalm 139:5 says, He has enclosed us from behind and before, and has laid His hand upon us.

As we reflect on God's faithfulness and power, as our roots go deeper into His love, an abiding trust will fill our hearts, and in our times of waiting, restlessness will be replaced by hope.

WHAT DO I PRAY FOR MY TEEN?

One frustration many moms have expressed is not knowing what to pray for their teenagers. "Sometimes I don't know specific needs of my boys because, at ages thirteen and sixteen, they tend to keep their thoughts private," said Joyce. One mom told me her son won't confide in her because he thinks all mothers are busybodies and tell their friends. He especially doesn't like her prying or quizzing him.

This isn't limited to adolescent boys, however. Karen says, "I have a fifteen-year-old daughter. Her needs now are so different than when she was small, but she often closes her bedroom door and tunes me out. So I have trouble knowing what's most important to pray for her."

Besides not feeling "clued in" to the particulars of our teen's life, fear can also hinder our prayers. "Sometimes the fear that my children are involved in something that will have long-lasting effect on their lives totally stops me in my tracks. It was much easier to control their lives when they were small!" (There's that control issue again.) Sometimes even to talk about—or pray about—our concerns for our teenagers makes them too real, and so we avoid taking our fears to the very One who can alleviate them.

PRAYERS FOR DISCIPLINE

As hard as it is, I believe one prayer we must pray for our children is that they will be caught when they're guilty. Even if you didn't start praying this in the early years, it's not too late. In the Psalms, David said that God's correction and discipline were the best things that could have happened to him because they taught him to pay attention to God's laws (Psalm 119:71). It's frightening to ask God to bring into the light anything in our lives that is in darkness, but mothers of teenagers have found it an effective way to pray. And it's a prayer God seems to answer quickly. Rather than being a negative, the answers to these prayers can convey a strong sense of God's reality and personal care—for us and our teens.

When Matt was in eighth grade, he went through puberty with a vengeance. "Our little boy disappeared and this angry teenager replaced him," says Kathy, his mom. He had always been an honor student, but suddenly his grades plunged. He started running around with a rough crowd. His relationship with his parents deteriorated, and they felt they were losing him.

Kathy began to pray that Matt would be caught whenever he was guilty, and the strangest things happened. He couldn't get away with anything. When he left campus without permission, school officials caught him and gave him detention. Then he was caught trying to buy marijuana. He sneaked out at night and was picked up by the police. Over the next several years, Kathy kept praying for him, and he continued getting caught. But he resisted efforts to help him.

"There were so many times I wanted to give up. I cried and asked God why. I said, "You made a big mistake, God. I was supposed to have a sweet Christian boy. Did you send us the wrong son?"

After much prayer—and financial incentive—Matt agreed to attend a six-week class for parents and teens called "Reaching the Heart of Your Teen." He slowly began to see how much his parents desired a good relationship with him and that they weren't giving up on him. Although he acted uninterested in class, he was listening, and the class became a turning point.

Matt's attitude toward his family improved. On his own initiative he chose to attend a youth group and to hang around with different friends. One Sunday as the family was riding home from church, Matt said, "It seems to me that men who know the Bible are wiser than men who don't. I'm going to start reading my Bible again."

Things are still stormy at times, but God is working—both in Matt and his parents. Kathy realizes she's grown more because of Matt than any person in her life. "Because of him I've learned what parenting and unconditional love are all about. It's easy to love my sweet child who always obeys and hugs me; it takes God's grace to love my hostile fifteen-year-old!"

PRAYERS FOR PROTECTION

A second, and almost instinctive, prayer we can pray for our teens is for protection. We won't always be with our teens at crucial times—as they travel home from out-of-town football games, as they go out on dates, as they attend parties. But God is there. It's as natural as breathing for a mom to pray God's protection for her child from the moment he picks up the car keys and heads for the highway.

We can also pray for protection of their purity. Libbi had always asked God to allow her kids to get caught when they did wrong, and she diligently prayed for God's protection and for her daughter's purity. When the family had to move to Michigan, Libbi's sixteen-year-old daughter became angry at God because she had to leave her friends and her church youth group.

However, she soon made friends and began dating again. But whenever she went out with guys, whether Christians or not, they seemed afraid to touch her. It was as if she had a barrier around her. She could see their reaction and knew why. It was all those prayers her mother prayed for her purity! Sensing God's protection ministered to her and kept her from getting into trouble in a new high school.

In fact, both of Libbi's kids know the wrong things they do will come to light, so they laugh about it. They candidly say, "If you're going to be my friend, let me tell you about my mom and how she prays!" As they have come to understand that God, in His love, stops them in their sin before it takes hold, they feel protected and cared for, and they share with their friends.

There are no instant solutions with teenagers. And undoubtedly we will have days when we question if God is working in their lives, and maybe even in our own. But we can trust our heavenly Father, whose very nature guarantees that His promises are true.

And He has promised that those who wait for Him will indeed gain new strength—and will soar like the eagles.

PUTTING FEET TO OUR PRAYERS

How can we pray for God's protection for our teens? Here are some ideas.

Pray for sins to be revealed. Get your courage up and say, "Lord, I ask You to deliver my son (or daughter) from evil according to Your Word. I pray that he will be caught when guilty so that his sins and foolishness can be brought into the light of Your presence, and so Your ways will be worth more to him than silver, gold, or the world's riches" (Psalm 119:71).

Pray for godly friends. Ask God to open your kids' eyes to the friends He has provided (Psalm 1; Proverbs 10:11). Pray for purity and that they will be saved for the right mate (2 Corinthians 6:14–17). If your child is hanging around with the wrong crowd, you can pray for those friends that they will be brought into the light as well.

Incubate your prayers. Many of the hopes and dreams we have for our teens need to "incubate," like an egg warmed by a mother hen. This mother-hen approach to prayer can help us in the tedious waiting when nothing is hatching.

Write down your deepest longings and prayers for your teens, and note the scriptures, if any, which reflect your petitions to God on their behalf. Then cut out your prayer request in the shape of an egg "to help dramatize the recognition that visible answers may be slow in coming"[8] and tuck it in your Bible. Then give the requests to God to work out in His timing, without your manipulation or striving. Each time you come across the egg, thank God for all He is going to do in the life of your child.

My daughter, Alison, and I were talking one day about the type of young man she hoped to marry. Without thinking, I began to jot down her dreams of the "ideal husband." After our conversation, together we committed her heart's desires to prayer. Then I tucked the list in my Bible near a favorite psalm. Each time I come across her prayer request, I lift it again to God and ask Him to provide for her just the man and marriage relationship He's planned.

Dial JE-333. My friend Dorothy is a mother to four children and a grandmother to eleven. When her eleventh grandchild received his driver's license, Corrie ten Boom told Dorothy to dial JE-333, the Lord's private telephone number, *often.* It's available twenty-four hours, every day. He says, "Call to Me, and I will answer you, and I will tell you great and mighty things, which you do not know" (Jeremiah 33:3).

Lord, thank You for the precious teenagers You've entrusted to my care.
Grant me Your unconditional love for them
and grace to faithfully intercede for them.
Lord, as I wait for You to answer all the petitions
that I have asked on their behalf, grant me patience
and a steady abiding in You. Let me hope in Your faithfulness
and find a resting place until the fulfillment comes.

In Jesus' name. Amen.

Great revivals always begin in the hearts
of a few men and women whom God arouses by His Spirit
to believe in Him as a living God.
They believe He is a God who answers prayer.
Upon their heart He lays a burden
from which no rest can be found
except in persistent crying unto God.

R. A. TORREY

CHAPTER EIGHT

A GREAT SPIRITUAL AWAKENING...LED BY YOUTH

"No eye has seen, no ear has heard,
no mind has conceived
what God has prepared
for those who love him."
1 CORINTHIANS 2:9 (NIV)

In the early morning hours, before the school bells ring, two mothers regularly take prayer walks around the Seoul Foreign School, which sits high on a hill in the middle of a bustling megacity. They pray for salvation for every teacher and every student who doesn't know Christ. They pray that each person who does know the Lord will be drawn closer to Him. They ask God to pour out His Spirit on the campus. They pray because they have a burning desire to see revival in their school, their nation, and around the world.

What are they praying for when they ask for "revival"? Perhaps you've been to a "revival service," but have you ever seen or experienced the fires of revival sweeping through your family or church? The dictionary tells us that *revival* means going from a depressed, inactive, disinterested state to becoming flourishing, active, and conscious of life.[1] Actually, that meaning isn't far off *revival* in a spiritual sense. "Revival is a sovereign act of God," says Dr. Bill Bright, "a divine visitation,...a time of personal humiliation, forgiveness and restoration in the Holy Spirit," and a time when the Holy Spirit is powerful and active in individual lives, churches, and the community at large.[2]

A season of spiritual refreshing or revival is accompanied by a harvest of new believers, where many people who have been in a dead or inactive spiritual state turn to God and experience new life in Christ. And wherever true revival has broken out, whether the Welsh Revival of the early 1900s or the Great Awakening, not only do hundreds and sometimes thousands of people come to know Christ, but Christians are renewed in their excitement and love for God.

Although revival initiates in the heart of God, intercessors prepare the way through prayer. The mighty revival in Ireland in the sixteenth century and the revival stirred by Jonathan Edwards's preaching in the eighteenth century both began in prayer. The fires of revival lit by the ministries of John Wesley, Charles Finney, and D. L. Moody originated in prayer.[3] Every revival in history was preceded by prayer—an earnest crying out to God to send His Spirit and to revive His people again.

Andrew Murray tells us that God sends revival in direct answer to prayer. "Those who know anything of the history of revivals will remember how often this has been proved—both larger and more local revivals have been distinctly traced to special prayer. In our own day there are numbers of congregations and missions where special or permanent revivals are—all glory be to God—connected with systemic, believing prayer. The coming revival will be no exception. An extraordinary spirit of prayer, urging believers to much secret and united prayer, pressing them to 'labor fervently' in their supplications, will be one of the surest signs of approaching showers and floods of blessing."[4]

He indicates that an increase of prayer is the surest sign that revival is coming, as God's people pray what His Spirit has revealed to them and prepare the way through intercession. That is what is so exciting about the current wellspring of interest in prayer—the hundreds of prayer groups forming in our country and around the world, the renewed interest in fasting, and the interest of children and teenagers in praying.

A GENERATION AT RISK

Why all this talk about revival? What does it have to do with moms?

Probably few would question the need for revival in America. All we have to do is look at what's happening with young people in the U.S. to see their desperate spiritual needs. Homicide and suicide are the leading causes of death among adolescents (with a 300 percent increase in suicide since the 1950s). And the age of those committing murder is getting younger every year.

Teen pregnancy has risen over 621 percent since 1940, which means that more than one million teenagers a year get pregnant. Of the 2,800 teens who get pregnant each day, 1,100 will have abortions.

The average age of first-time drug use is thirteen years old and getting younger.[5] Marijuana use among teens doubled in the early nineties.[6]

There is also an epidemic of depression in young people. Two decades ago the average age for the onset of a depressive episode was twenty-nine; now the average age for a serious depression is fourteen to fifteen.

A recent study showed that one-third of all high-school-age teens had stolen from a store, and two-thirds regularly cheated on exams. Several years ago a commission of business, education, and political leaders examining the problems of U.S. children and youth issued a report called "Code Blue" to emphasize the deadliness of the crisis. Their findings showed that the most basic cause of their suffering wasn't poverty or disease but self-destructive behavior.[7]

When I attended school in the fifties and sixties and started teaching in the late sixties, our problems ranged from gum chewing to note passing to spit-wad throwing. Now the problems in many schools in our country range from verbal and physical abuse of teachers to assault, rape, and drugs.

Dr. James Dobson called this generation of children and youth "a generation at risk." Josh McDowell said we would either lose this generation, or they would be the wellspring of the greatest spiritual awakening America has ever known. And that's just what they need: a spiritual awakening. I believe it won't take a trickle but a spiritual flood—a "breakthrough"—to reverse the moral slide. What is needed is not a minor adjustment but a radical change in the hearts of young people.

Adults in the U.S. need an awakening too. "Surely our nation needs a visit from our great God in heaven. We need another Pentecost! Many Christian leaders across the country are warning that unless America turns from her wicked ways, she will self-destruct.... Already a tidal wave of evil courses freely across our land," says Bright.[8]

And I believe an awakening is what God wants too. For those intercessors who keep their ears tuned to God's Spirit and seek to be used by Him, the words keep coming: God is going to move through the children and youth.

That's why the growth of groups of mothers committed to and focused on praying for children and teens and their schools is so encouraging. Thousands of these moms are lifting up their hands to God and pouring out their hearts like water before the face of the Lord on behalf of their children.[9] They are laying the tracks for God's power and presence to come. What's happening as moms pray for revival? Let's look first at a high school where God's Spirit is moving in response to prayer.

A YOUTH-LED REVIVAL

Beech High School in Hendersonville, Tennessee, is described by one substitute teacher as having a heavenly presence hovering over the campus. "There's a warmth and compassion in the students. At other schools I feel like I'm walking into a graveyard. Here it's like walking into the presence of God."[10]

For more than three years, students have raised daily, intensive prayers.

When you drive up to Beech, whether it's in the morning, at break, or lunch time, you see circles of ten or twenty or even sixty teenagers praying together, interceding for their classmates, for God's work in their own lives, for their community. Students also pray quietly in the halls between classes. They're not praying one special day a year around the flagpole, but every day!

In the band room before school on Mondays and Fridays, over two hundred teenagers lift their hands and voices to praise God—in a public high school. On Tuesdays and Thursdays, the room overflows with young people studying the Bible. No teachers leading, just students. On Wednesdays over two hundred kids show up in the choir room for the Fellowship of Christian Athletes meeting.

This student-led revival erupted at one high school and spread to the other high schools and middle schools in Hendersonville. The week I talked with Lee Brown, the leader of the Moms In Touch group for the high school, she and five other mothers were fasting and earnestly praying for God to do *more*—to pour out more of His Spirit and to bring more teens to Christ. They were earnestly interceding for more of the fires of revival for their community.

Three moms began interceding for Beech High School four years ago. They didn't pray just for blessings for their own children and their friends. God had put a unified vision on their hearts to pray for revival for the entire high school.

From the beginning the MITI group prayed for a standard of righteousness to be raised up at the school. When they asked that sin be exposed, Pandora's box opened. Drug abuse, gang activity, alcohol problems, and cheating—everything dark began to come to light. The principal brought in drug dogs. They became the only school in the county with a dress code. The school bought walkie-talkies for parents who strolled the campus to increase safety and to deter trouble, which provided another opportunity for them to quietly pray for the students and teachers as they walked the halls and grounds.

"We pray for our kids every day in our devotions, but we also pray for the lost. We want this school taken for Christ. We feel it's a key to the community, possibly the nation. When the fire hits, we want it to spread to high schools in other cities," says Lee.

One year the mothers made a prayer walk around the perimeter of the school every week for seven weeks. Four years ago they felt led to pray specifically that God would remove any teachers who were involved in the occult or who had a wrong influence. Without anyone complaining to the principal's office, twenty teachers left that summer. The next year, fourteen teachers left.

Three years ago youth pastors from more than half a dozen denominations in Hendersonville began supporting the revival and starting all-city youth rallies that included all denominations and races, and the renewal began to spread to other kids in the city.

The revival has affected many people, including the BHS principal, Mary Clouse. "I'm more approachable, calmer, and less stressed," she says. For the first time in her life, she has started studying Scripture and is deeply encouraged by the attitude change throughout the entire school.

As God moves at Beech High School, many teens have committed themselves to Christ. Many have been set free from alcohol and drug abuse. And the young people, mothers, youth pastors, and churches continue to pray. "We are expecting and asking for something that's never been seen on the face of the earth; we don't even know what it's going to look like. This is only the stirrings of revival, but we're excited," says Lee.

High schools in other areas are seeing signs of renewal and revival as well. At Poway High School in Southern California, moms have been praying for revival for thirteen years. They ask the Holy Spirit to help them remember to pray for revival every time they pick up their child, go to a school event, or drive by the high school. They are asking God to open the windows of heaven on the school.

And the window is opening. In the last year, many young people have come to Christ. At the "See You at the Poles" day, over two hundred teens gathered for prayer, praise, and worship at their school. More kids than ever are going to Youth for Christ and Student Venture weekend getaways. Christian teens are bolder in their faith and are praying for their friends. Even some people in the school administration are seeing the need for spiritual growth in the students.

"Revival starts in our own hearts, our homes, and in our school. We are seeing little pockets of revival and asking God for more," says Fern Nichols, who leads the group.

At Jenks High School in the Tulsa, Oklahoma, area, many people are combining prayer efforts—youth pastors, mothers, students, and ministries like Young Life and Fellowship of Christian Athletes (FCA). And this year God began moving in the FCA meetings.

"It all started with our officers going through the *Experiencing God* Bible study," says Kari. "This year we started praise and worship before FCA to invite the Holy Spirit to be there."

One night they were struck by the idea in Isaiah 57:15 that God, who dwells in the high and lofty, resides in those with broken and contrite spirits. That's when they prayed, "Lord, break us for our school; let us not be callous toward anyone." These teens are willing to be broken for those who need Christ's love and light, and they pray regularly for their lost classmates.

Coincidentally, the MITI group for Jenks High School had been praying for revival every week for two years. They prayed for many teens to see what a destructive path they are on, for evil to be exposed, and for Christian students and teachers to be bolder in their witness and to have a great burden for lost students.

Not only have they begun to see a harvest of young people committing their lives to the Lord every week in what used to be a nice social gathering, but new kids are coming to the FCA meetings. In one meeting thirty-five young men and women came forward to accept Christ, and over sixty came forward to recommit their lives to Christ.

WHAT ABOUT YOUR COMMUNITY?

What's happening at Beech High School, Poway, and Jenks can't help but encourage and inspire us. Perhaps it also makes you wonder what it would take to have a similar impact on the youth and high schools in your area.

"It takes the amassed prayer of many people to prepare the way of the Lord for nationwide revival," says Wesley Duewel. "But you or a few people can prevail for revival and see God work in power in a specific life, family, church, or perhaps even in a whole community. It is good to long for nationwide revival. But the more your prayer for revival is focused on a specific situation, the sooner you will probably see the answer to your prayers. Pray for both."[11]

Following Duewel's advice, we can learn from those praying for revival in their communities, and we can do likewise.

"Quit sitting on the bench just listening," Lee Brown advises us moms who want to see renewal. "Get one other person you can agree with in prayer, and start praying!" We can talk about prayer and say we believe God is strong and have much head knowledge about how important prayer is, but what we need to do is *pray*.

"If you want to see your children live for Christ and your school and community change, be committed to persistent prayer," she adds. "Prayer is one of our major weapons of warfare because the enemy is coming full force against our children and schools. We've got to use the weapon God has given us."

Like the California moms, as we drive by the schools and attend sports and music events, we can pray for God's Spirit to bless the teachers, students, and administrators. Think big and dream instead of limiting God; pray for a mighty revival.

And when we see God move, we shouldn't stop praying! Sometimes when things begin to change, we relax and let times of earnest prayer dwindle. But often that's when intercession is most needed. We must stay steadfast and persistent in prayer.

"We're finding that when God has moved greatly at the high school, spiritual pride can come in the Christian kids; apathy and complacency creep in. And when a standard of righteousness is raised up, Satan comes in like a flood," says Lee. They are seeing a trickle of gang activity and a rise in occult activity in kids who call themselves Satanists or Wicca followers. They find it important to pray continually with spiritual authority over the enemy and to study spiritual warfare. (For further study, see the recommended reading at the end of this book.)

A PERSONAL PERSPECTIVE

I too have seen how prayer lays the tracks for spiritual renewal—right in my own backyard. One summer, after having seen the power of prayer on our son Justin, I joined a group of women who met once a week for prayer.

"If you come, plan to stay for lunch," Jan, the leader, said. "We start at nine in the morning and usually pray until one or two, depending on how the Lord leads. Then we have a sandwich."

"Surely," I thought, "they can't pray that long. On a break before lunch maybe I can get a little work done." I worked full-time as a writer at the time and had a deadline for a magazine article, so I walked in, toting my red briefcase.

The group still chuckles about my briefcase accompanying me to the first few meetings—until I relaxed and joined in the second, third, and fourth hours of prayer. Jan, Kathleen, Kathy, Rose, and Kay had been praying together for years; I was the newly grafted branch. After an hour of study in two books on intercessory prayer, we had a time of worship and praise that brought us into God's presence, and often into brokenness and confession before the Lord.

Without a specific agenda, we just came to God and asked Him to lead us to intercede for whatever was on His heart. Among other things, He taught us more about being silent and waiting for Him to speak and about engaging in spiritual warfare.

We also shared with Him what was on our hearts and cast our cares on Him. Being moms, we usually had concerns for our high schoolers and college-age kids. So week after week, we were led back to praying for our children.

ENLARGING OUR HEARTS

But then God took us in a new direction; He enlarged our hearts to pray not only for our children's needs but for the young people of Oklahoma City, and eventually the whole generation, often called Generation X. The more we prayed, the wider our vision grew until we interceded at times for the youth in other nations. Week after week we cried out for revival and renewal in our lives and in America. Often when interceding for young people, we would weep over prodigal teens and pray for them to come home to God. Many of this young generation were on the edge of destruction—and definitely seemed to be on God's heart.

At the same time, in our city a community-wide Night of Praise was held one Friday night a month, led by a young man named Dennis Jernigan. Youth from all denominations, from high schools and colleges throughout Oklahoma and even Texas and Arkansas, were coming to worship God for several hours rather than going to their Friday night football games or parties. Along with our prayers, no doubt many other parents were praying for their teens, youth pastors were laboring and praying for them, and Jesus Himself was interceding day and night at the right hand of the Father.

What happened in our three years of Wednesday prayer summits? We had a growing sense that God was going to do something unique with this generation and that it was our privilege to pray for them. He gave us a real love for youth—both the lovely and unlovely ones.

Many times we didn't know specifically why we were praying for certain concerns in those hours together, but we felt the Holy Spirit was directing our intercession. "From our human, limited perspectives, it may seem that we initiate prayer," says Jennifer Dean in *The Praying Life*. "We feel a need or experience a desire to pray. As a result, we pray. Actually, our felt needs or desires to pray are a response to God's initiative."

"Before they call I will answer; while they are still speaking I will hear," the Lord says in Isaiah 65:24. And how God answered and spoke! Many of our own children were touched by God during the three years of prayer and since then. But the impact was far wider than our own families.

GROWING "THE GROUP"

After the Night of Praise gatherings, teens and college students started going to Jan and Johnny's house for fellowship. This gathering of youth grew and grew. Some of the young people were new believers, and others had grown up in Christian homes but were experiencing renewal. They met at our house every Tuesday night for Bible study. Then they wanted to start meeting every Saturday night for worship and praise, so Jan's home became the place.

Some of the youth went to the "Teen Boot Camps" held by Precept Ministries. These young men and women were growing by leaps and bounds, both in their knowledge of God's Word and in their relationship with Christ. They had a strong desire to walk in purity and serve God instead of going after material things or popularity.

We started seeing a peculiar breed of teen—more passionate about the Lord, more devoted to intercession for the lost. Of course we knew our prayers weren't the only reason God was drawing these young people. But when prodigal teens started flocking in, we saw God had been up to something all those weeping Wednesdays.

As we continued to pray, "The Group," as it was now called, grew larger. Jan and Johnny, who had a great heart for young believers, welcomed all who came, including teens with earrings and dyed hair. "The Group" finally outgrew their house, and they had to look for a space big enough to hold them.

At the same time, a group of adults who had been renewed in their relationship with God started meeting with Jan and Johnny, and out of months of prayer a common vision emerged for a church that would welcome renewal, that could equip the youth and offer them a place to grow and to minister, and would welcome the prodigals. The two groups merged with only about fifty adults and "The Group," the high school and college students, to form Bridgeway Church.

IGNITING THE PASSION

Each Sunday we come down the aisle at Bridgeway Church and see the worship team assembled. Charlie, Nathan, Brad, Brian, and the other musicians play keyboard, guitars, and drums. There are two adults on the team, but the worship definitely has a youth-friendly style, and the majority of the worship team are in their twenties.

Young people are on every row in the auditorium; over half of the congregation is younger than twenty-five years. From the beginning, high school and college men and women brought their friends and their parents. A minirevival has begun among these young people, and God is breaking the mold with them.

"God is igniting passion for Jesus in the hearts of young people in the heartland of America," says Josh Bottomley, a college student who ministers to teens. He sees God pouring out His presence, equipping young people to do right in a culture that is in moral decay. He also sees God giving them compassion for the lost, hurting, and broken. They've gone on mission trips to Honduras, Guatemala, Turkey, and South America. They've ministered to inner-city poor in Chicago, London, and Oklahoma City. They regularly minister at AIDS hospices, nursing homes, and engage in servant evangelism on their campuses. They hold a community-wide youth service twice a month where junior high, high school, and college kids from many campuses and churches gather.

This relatively new church has now grown to over one thousand members and spawned rapidly growing campus house churches on nine university campuses in the Oklahoma City area and several other nearby cities, in addition to numerous high school and adult house churches. An active house church for international students at the University of Central Oklahoma is expanding as students from China, Japan, and Middle Eastern countries come for university studies.

Intercessory prayer continues on Tuesdays and Sunday mornings as well as other times. We are asking God to pour out His Spirit. We are seeing the mere trickles of His Spirit and power, and we want to see a flood. As J. Edwin Orr, historian of revival worldwide, stated, "No great spiritual awakening has begun anywhere in the world apart from united prayer—Christians persistently praying for revival."[12]

THE CLOUD OF WITNESSES

As we pray, we mingle our prayers with others' prayers in our country and world, and with the prayers of the saints throughout the centuries—that great cloud of witnesses spoken of in Hebrews. How exciting to be a small part of what God is doing! How important to do my part to bring young people and the lost in our communities to the throne of grace.

"I must do the human side of intercession—utilizing the circumstances in which I find myself and the people who surround me," said Oswald Chambers. "I must keep my conscious life as a sacred place for the Holy Spirit. Then as I lift different ones to God through prayer, the Holy Spirit intercedes for them... And without that intercession, the lives of others would be left in poverty and in ruin."[13]

PUTTING FEET TO OUR PRAYERS

Keep these principles in mind as you pray for revival.

Engage in prevailing prayer. "The secret of prevailing prayer is simply to pray until the answer comes," says Wesley Duewel.[14] The length of time doesn't matter, he says; when the answer seems especially slow in coming, it's a test of our faith. For whom or what do you need to engage in prevailing prayer, perhaps sharing this need with others so they can support you?

If you are concerned about the youth in your city, could you commit to pray for revival until it comes—in your own home, church, or school?

Pray for this young generation. What's happening among our youth is a small picture of what's happening in other places. In New Zealand—a country where only 5 percent of the population is Christian and spiritual apathy characterizes the adults—children and youth are on fire for Christ, reports Deidre Chicken, who coordinates over three hundred Moms In Touch groups. Many prophetic words have been spoken concerning this generation of young people, but God is moving mightily among the youth. The greatest spiritual awakening the world has ever known could begin with them.

Lord, reveal Your plan, purpose, and vision
for the lives of children and youth, both in our church and city,
throughout our country and the world.
Strengthen their hearts and their commitment to Christ,
and grant that Your desires would become their desires.

In Jesus' name. Amen.

When a mother prays for her wayward son,
no words can make clear the vivid reality of her supplications....
She does not really think that she is persuading God
to be good to her son,
for the courage of her prayer is due to her certain faith
that God also must wish that boy to be recovered from his sin.
She rather is taking on her heart the same burden that God has on his;
is joining her demand with the divine desire.
In this system of personal life which makes up the moral universe,
she is taking her place alongside God
in an urgent, creative outpouring of sacrificial love.
Her intercession is the utterance of her life;
it is love on its knees.

HARRY EMERSON FOSDICK

CHAPTER NINE

PRAYING FOR PRODIGALS

If you know people who have wandered off
from God's truth, don't write them off.
Go after them.
Get them back and you will have rescued
precious lives from destruction
and prevented an epidemic of wandering away from God.

JAMES 5:19–20, THE MESSAGE

Sheryl was having a few last sips of coffee before heading for a women's ministry meeting when the phone rang.

"Mrs. Stewart, I need some information concerning your son Trent," the voice said.

"Whatever for? Has he been in some kind of accident?" she asked, her heart and mind racing.

"No, your son was arrested for possession and sale of illegal drugs, ma'am. He's going to need a good lawyer."

Sheryl leaned against the kitchen wall, frozen, trying to absorb the clerk's words: "...felony offense...could get five to ten years...bail set at $50,000..." As reality sank in, she became physically sick and then began sobbing.

In the first twenty-four hours, buckets of tears alternated with diarrhea. Sleep never came. But as morning dawned, even in her grief and anxiety about her son, she made a conscious decision to thank God for allowing Trent's arrest and for promising in His Word to work any circumstance, even this one, for good.

Less than a week before, during Trent's spring break from college, his parents had confronted him; they knew he was not only using drugs but selling them. "In all likelihood you're going to get caught," Sheryl had told him, pointing out the consequences. But her warnings fell on deaf ears.

The drug problems hadn't just begun; Trent had started with alcohol in high school and then moved on to marijuana. When his parents set boundaries, home became a battlefield. The more they tried to help him and hold him accountable, the more he resisted. Trent hated his parents' attempts to "control" him, and Sheryl dreaded getting up each morning to face the next skirmish.

"What did we do wrong?" Sheryl asked herself. She and her husband had brought up their kids in a Christian home, and both had served God in a ministry for years. They'd been involved in their kids' schools and sports. Family activities had been a priority. Sheryl had prayed for her kids daily on her own and in groups. Now everything was a constant fight.

In her anguish over Trent's rebellion, Sheryl was driven to her knees. As she increasingly poured out her heart to God, she realized she had never really known how to connect emotionally with God. The majority of her quiet time had been spent preparing to teach Bible studies and praying her list of needs and requests—almost like taking care of her "to-do" list.

CONNECTING WITH GOD

Sheryl changed her approach. She set aside her agenda and each morning entered into God's presence, just to experience His love and to connect with Him through a verse or two. Her verse for the day became a springboard for communion and ongoing prayer throughout the day. She began to understand what it meant to be still and know that He is God.

As she did, God moved her from focusing on all the negative things about her son to praising Him instead for the positive. Yet a constant mental, emotional, and spiritual battle raged. When Trent was rude or uncooperative, her temptation was to react. She had to consciously put on "a garment of praise."

She read her daily Bible passage until she felt the Holy Spirit stopping her at a verse.

Then she wrote that verse on two 3 X 5 cards—one went in a clear frame on the kitchen sink and the other on her car's dashboard—and asked God to teach her something about His character revealed in the verse. She would praise Him for that attribute all day. God, not the problem, was her focus.

As she got quiet before God and allowed Him to speak to her, she also looked for some truth about herself, her husband, and her children in the verse. Throughout the day she concentrated on that verse for each person, especially Trent. "I'd envision what it was going to be like when that verse was true about him. I'd thank God that it was going to happen in His timing, which brought me a tremendous peace," she says. By conscious discipline, she shifted her focus from his rebellious attitude to who he is as a child of God. The storms at home didn't dissipate right away, but over time her attitude changed, and she grew excited about what God was going to do.

One verse she chose was Ephesians 2:10, which says, "For we are God's workmanship, created in Christ Jesus to do good works, which God prepared in advance for us to do" (NIV). This verse reminded her that her children were God's workmanship—not hers. God's craftsmanship is impeccable, and He finishes what He starts. He had already prepared them for "good works," and she prayed they would respond to His leading.

PRAYER SUSTAINS US IN THE BLACKEST DAYS

Three years of praising God daily for who He is and how He was working in their family not only deepened her relationship with the Lord, it prepared her for what was ahead. On the outside, things got worse. Although Trent briefly stopped using drugs during the summer, he began using and selling drugs again when he went away to college.

Sheryl prayed and fasted. Out of this time came deep peace and confidence that God was still in charge and He wasn't letting go of Trent.

A few days later, Trent was arrested, and eventually he was sentenced to six months in jail. He recounted the next events in a letter he wrote from jail to the thirty people who had been praying for him.

> After I got arrested with multiple felony drug charges, I had no idea how drastically and quickly God would do his work. Before my arrest, my life was selling drugs. I was indifferent to my family and wasting my education. God rescued me from the depths of my despair by raiding my apartment and instantly cleaning out the physical impurities of my life. From that point God took care of me and began to work on my life. He let me out of jail, even though my bail was set at $50,000, brought me home to a spiritual family and friends, and gave me only six months in jail when I could have had years in prison.
>
> Jail was the most awesome time of my life. I had the privilege to leave this world and my old life and hang out with God for four months. He turned me completely inside out as I learned and experienced the strength of His perspective. My life is now His, and I cannot wait to see what He does with it. I know that it was the prayers of many which kept God so close to me and held my eyes on Him so I could see no other way. Sometimes I wish I could measure the power of prayer because I'm sure it's the greatest power we have. And the best gift we can give to anyone else. Thank you so much for your prayers. May the love of God touch your life as it has touched mine.

When Trent went back to college the next fall, he took bold steps. He shared with other students, his professors, and even those he'd sold drugs to, what God had done in his life. He has stayed sober and has been praying and fasting for his generation. He recognizes God's call on his life—that he has indeed "been prepared for good works."

LOVE ON ITS KNEES

"As a mother, I must faithfully, patiently, lovingly and happily do my part—then quietly wait for God to do His," said Ruth Bell Graham in *Prodigals and Those Who Love Them,* reflecting on her experience with her sons. Much of our part is praying—that "love on its knees"—all the time releasing our children to God and letting the Holy Spirit minister to them instead of our trying to be their personal Holy Spirit. Maybe you thought you had already entrusted your child to God—until your prodigal made a few more wrong choices. Facing that situation, most of us take things back into our own hands to try to fix things. And when our prodigals continue making mistakes, we find ourselves torn: How much should we help? Why is this taking so long? Can I really let go and trust God with this child?

"I'm a praying mom out of necessity," says Lydie. "I'd be a patient in the local mental hospital if I were not."

Her son Carson made some bad choices which led to legal consequences. Although he was able to attend summer school two hours away, his life was restricted because of court-enforced community service, restricted driving privileges, and working.

Late on a Monday afternoon, Lydie got a call from Carson, who had hurt his back again and was in tears. Being a tall guy, he had complained of back pain for several years. When the pain flared up, the doctors called it a pulled muscle and treated him with pain pills and muscle relaxants. This time the pain was so severe he'd gone to the emergency room. He'd missed class and was frantic because he'd already missed the limit and was in danger of failing the course. Lydie tried to comfort and encourage him, but he was out of control emotionally.

"The mother in me wanted to drive the two hours to Atlanta and hold my boy, but God kept whispering to my heart to let him go. I wept as I told God, 'Okay, I'll get out of the way so You can work.'" It took everything she had to say those words, to release Him to God. She decided to ride to the church with Stan and work while he was in a deacons meeting, knowing that if she stayed home, she might call him or drive to Atlanta.

When they returned home that evening, Stan called Carson and asked if he could pray with him over the phone. Previously Carson had responded to any such requests by mocking them.

"This night was different," says Lydie. "He had nowhere to go but Jesus."

After his dad prayed for his physical and spiritual healing, Carson told him he loved him.

"To some, that's not a big deal, but we are beginning to see dust in the air as the walls of self are shaking a little! We continue to claim Carson for Jesus with our very fiber. God is faithful to answer when I am willing to get out of the way and let Him get next to our son!"

Sheryl's and Lydie's experience reminds me of the poem "Broken Dreams":

As children bring their broken toys
With tears for us to mend,
I brought my broken dreams to God
Because He was my friend.
But then instead of leaving Him
In peace to work alone,
I hung around and tried to help
with ways that were my own.
At last I snatched them back and cried,
"How can you be so slow?"
"My child," He said, "what could I do?
You never did let go."

UNKNOWN

When we trust God enough to leave our broken dreams with Him, "not only do we eventually get them back gloriously restored, but are also handed a surprising plus," says Catherine Marshall. "We find for ourselves what the saints and mystics affirm, that during the dark waiting period when self-effort had ceased, a spurt of astonishing spiritual growth took place in us. Afterwards we have qualities like more patience, more love for the Lord and those around us, more ability to hear His voice, greater willingness to obey."[1]

THE LORD OF THE BREAKTHROUGH

Praying for prodigals calls for a special kind of listening to God and not leaning on our own understanding or formulas. Whereas we rush in to pray what we think God should do, He may have a different plan. And it often comes when we are most discouraged.

Every time Gina prayed for her son Aaron, the word *flood* came to mind. But she ignored it and continued claiming scriptures for her son and asking God to please do something about the guns and drugs Aaron bought and sold and the bad friends he hung around with. But the gap between Aaron's behavior and Scripture's promises was so great that she grew more discouraged. One day she got honest with God. "I've prayed and confessed this thousands of times, but I guess I don't believe it anymore. You know, Lord, I'm tired of praying these things. I want to follow Your will and be a good prayer warrior, but I'm more depressed when I finish praying about Aaron than when I start!"

It was as if God said, "I was waiting for you to lay down your way of doing this." Isaiah 55:8 immediately came to mind: "'For My thoughts are not your thoughts, neither are your ways My ways,' declares the LORD." Her way didn't appear to be working, so she started thinking about God's ways and that recurring word *flood.*

As she traced *flood* throughout the Bible, she saw a pattern: When the whole earth had become a stronghold of the devil, God opened the floodgates of heaven (Genesis 6:5; 7:10). "As waters break out, God has broken out against my enemies," David says in 1 Chronicles 14:11 (NIV). In fact, David calls Him the Lord of the Breakthrough, as in the breaking forth of waters. Again, in Nahum 1:8, God's vengeance on His enemies—here, the city of Nineveh—is described as a flood: "with an overwhelming flood He will make an end of Nineveh" (NIV).

What she thought God could do—her "expecter"—expanded. She realized He can break a stronghold that appears impregnable. Sometimes He works little by little; step by step a person comes closer to God. But sometimes God comes in like a flood to change lives. She knew her son didn't need just to inch closer to God; he needed a radical change.

"Don't look for any improvement until there is a complete change," the Spirit seemed to say. "I will change him in one day; I will lift Him up and put him in the place I've called him."

"How are you going to reach him?" Gina asked. Aaron wasn't going to church or even asking for prayer.

"Just keep praying for the breakthrough, for the flood in Aaron's life, and trust Me," came the reply.

Seven months passed with no change. Then one night, the Lord did bring a flood; He flooded Aaron's room and his heart with His presence. He gave him a clear vision of what his life would be like within a year if he didn't turn back to Him. What Aaron saw scared him so badly he couldn't move; he just shook and began to pray. He fell to his knees before God and wept for his sins. Later, Aaron went to the phone and asked a friend to come and pray with him.

When he called his mom the next day, he was a different person. She could hardly believe what had happened. Now, eight months after his "breakthrough," Aaron attends Bible school, teaches a Bible study for over thirty-five teens each week, and spends much time in prayer. "I just wanted him to stop doing drugs and go to church. I didn't think he'd be running to God with these intense prayer burdens," says Gina. God did exceedingly more than what she asked.

This concept of breakthrough has its parallel in nature. "When a dam is erected in a mountain valley, its construction may take many months. Then the water begins accumulating behind the dam, which can take months or even a year or longer. But when the water level reaches the right height, the sluice gates are opened, water begins to turn the generators, and there is tremendous power." Maybe something like this happens in the spiritual realm, says Wesley Duewel. "As more and more people unite in prayer or as the prevailing person prays on and on, it seems as if a great mass of prayer is accumulated until suddenly there is a breakthrough and God's will is accomplished.… Prayers prayed in the will of God are never lost but are stored until God gives the answer."[2]

DON'T QUIT TOO SOON

Have you been heaping up prayers for a prodigal without seeing an inch of movement? Are you weary and tempted to give up? Remember what Jesus said in Matthew 7:7? "Ask, and it shall be given to you; seek, and you shall find; knock, and it shall be opened to you," He wasn't suggesting a one-time "Please God, do this.…" He tells us to ask and keep on asking, to seek and keep on seeking, to knock and knock persistently!

Florence Chadwick might also have something to say to us about this.

In 1952 Florence Chadwick was set to swim the channel from Catalina Island to the California coast. She'd been the first woman to swim the English Channel, so long-distance swimming wasn't new to her. But this day the water was chilling, the fog so thick she could barely see the boats around her, the waters infested with sharks so that her trainers on the accompanying boats had to use rifles to drive them away.

For fifteen hours she swam, braving the numbing cold and the sharks. Finally she could go no farther, and she asked her trainers to lift her into the boat. They encouraged her to keep swimming since they were close to land, but all she could see was the fog.

Florence quit. And when she got into the boat, she saw she was only a half-mile from the shore. She had stopped within sight of her destination.

Sometimes we become shrouded in a fog of discouragement or weariness, and it looks like things will never change. But press on. Keep praying. Gather other moms to help you persevere. That breakthrough may be just around the corner.

As Andrew Murray says, "Prayer must often be 'heaped up' until God sees that its measure is full. Then the answer comes. Just as each of ten thousand seeds is a part of the final harvest, frequently repeated, persevering prayer is necessary to acquire a desired blessing.... Real faith can never be disappointed. It knows that to exercise its power, it must be gathered up, just like water, until the stream can come down in full force."[3]

PUTTING FEET TO OUR PRAYERS

Maybe you feel like the mom who told me, "I've run out of ways to pray for my prodigal, and he's still running from God and headlong toward destruction." I hope the following ideas will encourage you and help you to persevere in your prayers.

Pray a "hedge of thorns." Hosea's wife, Gomer, was adulterous and continually running after other lovers. Hosea said, "Therefore I will block her path with thornbushes; I will wall her in so that she cannot find her way. She will chase after her lovers but not catch them; she will look for them but not find them" (Hosea 2:6–7, NIV).

When a young person doesn't have the wisdom to see the destructive path he is on, we can pray, "Lord, I ask You to a build a hedge of thorns around (name) to separate him from any influence not ordained by You. I pray that those who would lure him into evil will lose interest and flee from him. I also pray that You will hedge him in so he won't be able to contact those who are out of Your will." Just as Hosea's actions caused Gomer's lovers to depart, this prayer can form a double hedge—a hedge within and without. As my friend Karen says, "There's nothing wrong with frustrating evil!"

This prayer is not guaranteed to change the will of our children since God gives us free will, but God can remove wrong influences. When that happens, we pray our children will turn to God in their frustration!

Don't discount the ministry of tears. Perhaps there are times when your words are exhausted; all you can do is weep over your child. Know that your tears are not in vain. Through the ministry of your tears, the Holy Spirit makes intercession: "If we don't know how or what to pray, it doesn't matter. He does our praying in and for us, making prayer out of our wordless sighs, our aching groans" (Romans 8:26–27, THE MESSAGE). In fact, a mother of a prodigal could have written: "You've kept track of my every toss and turn through the sleepless nights, each tear entered in your ledger, each ache written in your book" (Psalm 56:8, THE MESSAGE).

O Lord my God! Teach me how to know Your way
and in faith to learn what Your beloved Son has taught:
"He will avenge them speedily." Let Your tender love,
and the delight You have in hearing and blessing Your children,
lead me implicitly to accept the promise that
we may have whatever we ask for,
and that the answer will be seen in due time.
Lord! We understand nature's seasons; we know how to wait
for the fruit we long for. Fill us with the assurance that
You won't delay one moment longer than is necessary,
and that our faith will hasten the answer.

ANDREW MURRAY

Do you have loved ones who live a great distance away?
Perhaps a son or a daughter who is away at school?
Between my mother and me was the entire state of Wisconsin,
and beyond that the vastness of Lake Michigan.
Yet in prayer we both sensed a oneness
that transcended the miles that separated us.
God is not limited to space, as we are.
He is able to reach down and give the unifying sense of His presence
not only to people sitting beside us in the room
but to individuals who are separated by continents.

EVELYN CHRISTENSON

CHAPTER TEN

WHEN YOUR CHILD MOVES AWAY FROM HOME

I have no greater joy than this,
to hear of my children walking in the truth.
3 JOHN 1:4

They're on their own now.

Your grocery bills are less, your loads of laundry are fewer, and occasionally a phone call is actually for *you*.

Your children aren't the only ones who experience culture shock when they move away from home for the first time—whether they're heading for college, a trade school, or a full-time job. For the first time, your kids aren't under your roof, aren't underfoot, and aren't under your "wing." No more talks in the evenings about their four tests coming up, Friday night's date, or not being nominated for Homecoming Queen. No more serendipitous opportunities for a heart-to-heart conversation when you catch them in a talkative mood. As one mother said, "It's hard to talk about the heart issues with our son when he's hundreds of miles away. We get general information—where's he's going for spring break or what he's doing on the weekend—but it's difficult to know the specifics of his life."

It's tempting—and candidly, maybe a bit of a relief—to think, "They're on their own now," and let both our communication and prayer support dwindle. Yet Dr. James Dobson calls the years from sixteen to twenty-six the critical decade because young people are making decisions that will affect their whole lives: deciding on a career, perhaps choosing a mate, settling into a lifestyle. Will they throw away their faith, as many young people do in these years, or will they become more committed to Christ and develop a stronger faith?

College-bound kids certainly face many challenges—academic, financial, moral, and spiritual. Many enroll in classes that teach secular humanism and challenge their faith. National policy considers eighteen-year-olds as independent of parents. Thus, by law colleges can't send grades to parents, can't notify them if their child has AIDS or is pregnant.[1]

Many young adults spiritually "hang in the balance" in these years. The majority of young men and women go through a crisis of belief in which they decide if they accept the faith of their parents as their own. As they are exposed to philosophies and belief systems that range from secular humanism to New Age, Islam to agnosticism, their faith will be tested.

How can our prayers go with them as they leave home?

STANDING IN THE GAP

When my young friend Brent was accepted at the State Math and Science School, he had to leave home his junior year and move to the University of Oklahoma campus, an hour away from his family. Brent was very bright, and this was a terrific opportunity. His mom, Kathy, was in a prayer group that covered Brent in prayer every week. They asked for God's protection for his mind, praying for his faith to grow stronger and not be smothered by intellectualism.

Since Brent came home every weekend, his mom and dad could discuss things with him and stay in close touch. He thrived at the school and by the end of the year won a scholarship to M.I.T., Massachusetts Institute of Technology, in Boston. At eighteen Brent moved over sixteen hundred miles away from his family and church in Oklahoma.

His parents kept in touch as much as possible, but they worried that

Brent had no Christian fellowship. He tried to start a Bible study, but no one showed up. He joined a fraternity but still was lonely for spiritual fellowship.

In the spring semester, however, a classmate befriended Brent and asked him to meet over coffee to discuss spiritual matters. Glad to have a friend to hang out with, Brent agreed. They got together several times that week and were joined by two other men his friend brought along. Brent soon started going to church with them. His parents were encouraged that he had some spiritual support.

One week when Brent called home, he told his mom the men had come to his room every night that week. They had also assigned him a "discipler" and were teaching him about bringing people into the kingdom. Some of what Brent shared of their teachings made Kathy uneasy. It didn't line up with the Bible. So the next day Kathy called her pastor and shared her concerns, including that these men had met with Brent three-on-one for a week. She asked if he knew anything about this church.

He called a pastor friend of his in Boston to check it out and two days later got back with Kathy, telling her it was known throughout the area as a cult.

"When I got off the phone, my heart was pumping," Kathy said. "I tried to call John and a few friends, but I couldn't get anyone. I felt like God was saying, 'Talk to Me about this!'" Kathy went right to prayer, and ten minutes later a friend called. She told him their concerns for Brent and asked if he knew anything about the group. He happened to know a young man who had just come out of the cult, so he had him call Kathy to give her more information.

The news wasn't good. "The group is totally dominating. Everyone has a discipler, who tells you where to live, where to work, how to spend your money, and who to marry," the man said. "Once you're in, it's very hard to get out. Tell your son to stay away from it."

Kathy desperately wanted to pray about it more before calling Brent, but she had to drive her daughter's cheerleading group to an overnight meet in Tulsa. As soon as they hit the road, the girls were asleep, giving Kathy two hours to intercede for Brent and to ask that angels of protection be with him.

"I wanted to fly up there and say, 'Hold it! Stop!' and yet that's what prayer can do. We can communicate with the Creator of the universe," says Kathy. As she drove, Ephesians 6 came to mind, and she prayed that Brent would be totally suited out with the armor of God for this spiritual battle.

The next day, Brent's dad sent him a message via e-mail: "Son, don't join anything that you don't know all about." That night Kathy and John's Bible study group and other friends prayed for Brent—at the very time the group was asking for his decision about joining them.

Brent called his parents the next night. He had told the guys he felt that God was telling him not to pursue this church any further.

"How do you know it's God?" they had quizzed.

"I just know," he had answered. Although they tried to convince him that Jesus recommended his leaving his father and mother to join them, Brent stayed firm. Kathy's and John's prayers, and the prayers of their friends, had been clearly answered.

Now whenever Kathy feels helpless, being so far away from their son, God reminds her again, "You stand in the gap here, and I'll take care of him there." He reminds her He's omnipresent—as present in Massachusetts as Oklahoma. He reminds her He's omniscient—that His knowledge includes everything that has existed or will ever exist—and yet He invites her to pray and make known her requests!

LONG-DISTANCE CALLS

Going to a military academy had been Brian's dream for years, but it was just that—a dream. His father had died after a long illness in Brian's junior year of high school. As the months went by, Brian's dream of going to a military academy was also dying as there was no word from any of the academies to which he'd applied. His hope and faith were withering. However, his mother continued to pray for him, specifically for an opening at West Point, for godly young men around him, and for direction for his life.

Facing reality, Brian finally turned to firefighting and enrolled in a local community college. But on April 26, 1995, the office of their local congressional representative called and asked for Brian.

His mother, Marilyn, stood watching him as he took the phone. "I knew something big was up, but I didn't have a clue what. I watched his posture become more erect, then he hung up and announced that an offer of admission to West Point was coming." In nine weeks, Brian was on a plane to New York to begin his army officer career.

Marilyn was thrilled with her son's opportunity but nervous about the temptations he'd face away from home. He wasn't walking with Christ and only went to church when it was expected. She'd be on the West Coast, he'd be on the East Coast. Would he return to the values she'd taught him?

"Lord," she prayed, "West Point is so far away. Can I find another Christian mom, somewhere, to pray with me?" He was just waiting for her to ask. Marilyn soon found two West Point moms—one in the next town and the other about twenty minutes away. Now Marilyn e-mails encouraging scriptures and prayer requests back and forth to one mother. She and the other mother pray and encourage each other over the phone. Although the moms have prayed with her about many things for Brian, they consistently centered on her heart's desire: for Christian cadets around him.

After his freshman year, two cadets came to visit Brian at home over summer leave. One cadet walked in wearing a West Point Fellowship of Christian Athletes T-shirt and shared stories about how he felt led by God to hitchhike halfway home during leave and witness along the way. The other cadet's grandmother is in a nursing home one mile from Brian's house. Both young men love the Lord.

The biggest answer to prayer, however, has been Brian's change of heart. Instead of growing away from God, he's grown closer to Him.

TURNING TO GOD'S WORD

God's Word is a lamp to our feet and a light for our path, Psalm 119:105 tells us. We know it can give our kids the wisdom they need for decisions, and the discernment to know the truth from false philosophies they may be exposed to on college campuses. God's Word can bring them freedom and keep them from sin. But we can't nudge them, remind them, or take them to Bible studies when they're away from home. For many teens, it's a time they drift away from God's Word.

Sharon was concerned about her son Joseph. He hadn't walked with the Lord for several years and was spiritually adrift. Having attention deficit disorder (ADD), he struggled in high school and went into a deep depression and rebellion his senior year.

After he graduated from high school and began to come out of his depression, he started attending junior college. Sharon prayed Psalm 119:36–37 for him: "Turn Joseph's heart toward your statutes and not toward selfish gain. Turn his eyes away from worthless things; preserve his life according to your word" (NIV). She prayed all that year that the Lord would turn his heart toward His Word so the truth could set him free. She also asked God to provide a spiritual mentor.

For several years Sharon prayed without seeing any change in her son. Then God sent a spiritual young woman into Joseph's life, and one by one he gave up all of his other friends who weren't a good influence. She had thought the mentor she had prayed for would be a youth pastor, but God surprised her!

One day out of the blue Joseph came in and said, "Mom, I've decided to read the Bible all the way through." He plunged right in with Genesis, and by the time he made it through Leviticus, they knew he was serious. She began to see miraculous changes in his life. His grades came up, and he was accepted at Baylor University. The day before he left, as they sat at the breakfast table, Sharon shared what a blessing his spiritual growth was to her and his dad. He told her, "Mom, my life began to change when I started reading the Bible." She was then able to tell him how she'd prayed for years that his heart would turn toward God's Word.

God can show us how to target our child's need with just the right scripture, even if we aren't with our kids to see what's going on. I have several verses that are standard fare in my prayer time for my college-age son, Chris, but a few months ago I felt a need for new direction from the Lord. So I asked God to reveal a special verse that would be right in line with His heart toward our son.

One night soon after, I had a dream. In it, Chris was standing beside me, holding a Bible and pointing out a verse as if to say, "That's me, Mom." The verse was Acts 17:28: "For in him we live and move and have our being" (NIV). I sensed God was telling me that the truth about Chris is that he lives and moves and has his being in Christ, and that I should pray he would realize this. And the Spirit continues to point me back to this verse—to remind me to continue praying and to remember that He is the One who began a good work in Chris and He will complete it!

CHANGING A CAMPUS

Colleges and universities are the training grounds for the next generation of teachers and leaders. What happens on these campuses will influence our children, not only when they attend college but as society's ideas are shaped there. As Gary Bauer said, "Most of our children arrive in college with high ideals but sadly find that traditional ideas are mocked or even shunned. On too many campuses, the absence of truth is the only absolute truth. Secular universities from Dartmouth to Stanford have institutionalized programs promoting sexual license. Events like…the 'Condom Rating Contest' include such promotional features as a pamphlet urging students to try them out 'by yourself, with a partner, or partners. Be creative. Have fun. Enjoy.'"[2]

Can prayer make a difference on college campuses? Those who pray find it does. "Through prayer God is changing our campuses. Our group prays from Jeremiah 33:8–9 that God will cleanse our campuses and make them institutions that bring Him renown, joy, praise and honor," says Lydia.

One problem on a particular campus they were praying for was the widespread use of drugs and alcohol in the dorms. The young people who wanted to abstain were constantly around others who abused the substances. Without ever going to the administration to ask for changes, the group began to ask God for a change.

As a result, this university instituted a wellness dorm, which is substance-free, so that students have the option to live with others who want an alcohol- and drug-free environment. They also prayed about a class on human sexuality that promoted antifamily values and used an extremely offensive textbook. The class was temporarily dropped, then restructured, and a new professor, a Christian counselor, was chosen to teach the class—a man who had impacted one of the prayer group members years before in another state.

College Moms In Touch also have prayed that godly values and integrity will be upheld and that dishonesty and compromise will not be tolerated among the administration and faculty. At a university they prayed for, a coach had been lying and covering up the truth in a campus incident. In answer to their prayers, the university president's response in a local newspaper read: "Those in high positions have an obligation to tell the truth."

An Illinois college group prayed that honesty be the standard and that anything done in darkness be exposed. When a university president came under investigation for accepting questionable funds, the mothers asked God to bring the truth forward and that if this was a real violation, he would be removed from the position. Before any information could be released in the investigation, the president suddenly resigned.

As mothers pray seemingly impossible prayers for college students and campuses, God is changing both. Sometimes the answers even show up in black and white in the university newspaper.

PRAYING FOR PRACTICAL NEEDS

When kids know their mothers are praying weekly, they are more likely to share a need and even ask for prayer. And as we pray about very practical things like their getting the classes they need or choosing the right major or making the right job decision, their faith is built up by seeing that God is real and actively involved in their lives.

When Terry's daughter left home to transfer to a different college, she couldn't get into any of the classes she needed for graduation. She asked the MITI group to pray that she'd get the necessary classes. The girl's adviser suggested she sit in on other classes and see if openings developed. She sat in on seven classes waiting for openings. Two days later, she called to thank her mom and the prayer group for "open doors;" she was registered for all four classes she needed.

If you have a child in college or living on his own for the first time, you might consider the following ways to support your child long distance. (If you have more than one child in college, you have my prayers!)

Start a college group of praying moms. This year three of us college moms from our church began meeting at my house to pray for our five students. Within a week, another college mother joined us. Every week a new mother joins, eager to pray for her college son or daughter, so that now we're interceding for the University of Oklahoma, Oklahoma State University, University of Central Oklahoma, University of Texas, and Massachusetts Institute of Technology campuses. I encourage you—if you start it, they will come! We college moms know we're not in control, and we want to see God work in the lives of our young adults.

If you're uncertain how to start, ask God to bring another college mom to you. All you need is one. Your students don't even need to attend the same college.

You can also put a notice in your church bulletin and in other local churches that says: "Moms In Touch College Prayer Groups—Make an eternal difference in your college student's life through prayer. To join a group of moms near you, call (your name and number). All college moms are welcome, whether your student attends college in or out of state, a Christian or secular college, community college or technical school."

You can also check with your local MITI area coordinator or with Christian high schools for the mothers of graduating seniors.

Find a central meeting place where no one has to drive more than fifteen minutes, purchase the MITI booklet and request college resources, get started, and pray![3]

Subscribe to the campus newspaper where your child attends college. The campus paper is a great source of information about what's going on and, therefore, can give you specific needs to pray about. You might even get to see answered prayers!

Give a birthday gift of prayer. On your son's (or daughter's) birthday, spend an hour or more praying just for him and his needs. Ask God to pour out His Spirit and bless your child in ways that will reveal His love. Include a message about your "gift of prayer" in the card you send.

Some specific prayers for children on their own include:

1. That they will desire to please the Lord in every area of their lives (1 Corinthians 10:31)

2. That their relationship with God will grow and they'll seek His will for their lives (Philippians 1:9–10)

3. That they will find a church home and fellowship with other believers (Hebrews 10:24–25)

4. That they will hold fast to the basic Christian values they have been taught (Proverbs 4:1–2; Colossians 2:8)

5. That they will have wisdom and discernment as they choose their classes, jobs, and friends (Proverbs 3:3–6; Colossians 1:9)

Although our young adults aren't under our wings anymore, they can be securely under His wings as we pray.

Lord, our children are taking flight as they leave home.
With Your grace, we have given them "roots."
Now, Lord, may the winds of Your Spirit be their inspiration and guide
as they journey into adulthood.
At every critical juncture and decision,
whether it's which major, course, or job to choose,
may they turn to You and experience firsthand Your faithfulness.

In Jesus' name. Amen.

I know not by what methods rare,
But this I know: God answers prayer.
I know not if the blessing sought
Will come in just the guise I thought,
I leave my prayer to him alone
Whose will is wiser than my own.

ELIZA M. HICKOK

CHAPTER ELEVEN

PRAYING FOR YOUR CHILD'S MATE

Trust in Him at all times, O people;
Pour out your heart before Him;
God is a refuge for us.
PSALM 62:8

We pray for it. We expect it. We agree that, in principle at least, it's a good thing.

We did it ourselves, and it didn't turn out half-bad.

But when it comes right down to it—when our darling son or our princess daughter decides to marry—how do we react?

We wonder, "Will he provide well enough for her?"

"Will she see that he needs to come home occasionally, by himself, so we can really visit?"

"Will they ever spend Christmas here?"

And, perhaps, in our heart of hearts—"Could anyone really be worthy of my child?"

Other than their salvation, is there any area in which we feel a greater need for prayer and God's leading and protection than in our children's selection of a life partner?

I find mothers need so much encouragement in this area. We worry that we didn't start praying about their mates soon enough. (Who had time to think about it when he had colic?) We question how to pray when we have serious misgivings about the person they've selected. (Lord, is it too much to ask that this boy join the French Foreign Legion instead?) We agonize when a baby precedes the marriage. (Lord, how do I pray now?)

Praying for our children's future mate brings with it a host of concerns—praying that God will lead them to the right person, praying their purity will be protected until marriage, praying they will be prevented from the wrong mate (remember the "Girlfriend from the Pit"?). As I have prayed about God's will for my kids regarding marriage, it has encouraged me to know that God has been answering these prayers from moms for a long time.

LONG-DISTANCE PRAYERS

During World War II, Bill Starr was in the navy. After weeks at sea, his ship docked in Panama City for a two-week stay. As the men began lining up their duty and liberty hours, they planned how they could "shack up" with the local women.

"I thought it was my chance to go out and become a man," Bill says. "I was about twenty at the time and had never slept with a woman. All the talk on ship was if you hadn't had sex with a woman, you weren't a real man. So this was going to be my baptism into manhood."

When Bill's liberty came, he eagerly joined the rush off the ship. However, shortly after arriving in town, he passed an alley where a man and a woman were openly engaged in intercourse. He was so repulsed by this public display that he became physically ill and turned around and went straight back to the ship. Bill had had enough.

He immediately sensed this was direct, heavenly intervention. Why? "Because I was hellbent on another direction, and I knew about my mother's prayers for me in this." In every letter she told Bill about praying for him and his five brothers every day and how confident she was that her Lord would keep her sons. She prayed constantly for protection of all kinds—physical, spiritual, and moral.

At that time in his life Bill would have termed himself a "nominal Christian," but this experience convinced him of the reality of God's love for him and of the long-distance impact of intercessory prayer. "It works," he says. "There's no distance factor in praying for someone. You're just as much in the presence of that person as if you were standing there speaking with him."

For years his mother had also prayed for the Holy Spirit to direct her children to the ones He wanted them to spend their lives with, the ones that fit with His plan for their future and purpose. "We know there are many people we could love in life, but mother was convinced that God had handpicked someone for each of us, and she never wavered," Bill says.

Before and during his service years, Bill dated a particular young woman. She was a fine person, and they had a serious relationship. But Bill had the subtle conviction it wasn't the right one and finally stopped seeing her.

At age twenty-three when he got out of the service, Bill attended Wheaton College. One summer while he was speaking at a youth conference in Wisconsin, he met the conference nurse, Ruth. "The day we met I had that wild sense that I had just met the person God wanted me to marry. I had never encountered that feeling before."

In fact, as he would later learn, Ruth and he simultaneously sensed that God had prepared them for each other and that God had honored both of their mothers' prayers. Married for forty-seven years until Ruth's death, they had a unique relationship. As director of the International Young Life ministry, Bill spent three decades in constant travel away from his family. Ruth could have resented his being away and her having the main responsibility for parenting their four children, but she was very supportive of Bill's work and loyal to what they sensed was God's leading.

"When I'd come home from a long ministry trip, I'd enter a pool of peace instead of conflict. It was a relief to come home and find her supportive and encouraging," Bill says. They were God's gift to each other—and the fulfillment of their mothers' prayers.

Praying for the Right Person

Praying for the right mate also has the flip side of asking God to protect our children from the wrong one. What happens when we see a red flag in a relationship our child is serious about? What can we do when we truly believe the relationship is not God's best?

That's the situation in which my friend Terry found herself. When her daughter, Susan, started dating Jared, Terry and her husband were eager to get to know him. But as the relationship developed over several months, flags went up. They saw him dominating her and criticizing her. They felt Susan was doing all the giving and he all the taking in the relationship. Having seen so many marriages where a spouse brings out the worst or holds the partner back spiritually, they were concerned for Susan.

To add to their doubts, Jared wasn't interested in spending much time with the family. When he picked Susan up for a date, they left quickly. When they tried to get to know him better, he was evasive. As their relationship with him faltered, they began to pray for guidance.

After prayer with her husband, Gil, and fasting to seek God's direction, Terry sat down with her daughter and pointed out what they had noticed and were concerned about. Although the couple was on the verge of engagement, Terry and Gil asked that they stop seeing each other for a while to examine if marriage was the right move.

Although Susan didn't see the concerns her parents did, she respected the sincerity of their feelings and said, "If those problems are really there, I need to see them too." She was willing to step back and honor her parents' advice. Jared also honored their request for a time apart.

Terry felt led to fast for twenty-one days, asking God to work in each of their hearts—hers included—and show them what He wanted. Before long, Jared called and asked if he could meet with them alone, without Susan. "I really care about Susan and don't want to lose her," he explained. "I see some areas where I need to change. Could we get together each week and talk?"

So they began meeting each week with Jared. He was eager to know what he needed to work on and genuinely receptive to their input. They, in turn, learned about his past and his family. Being one of five boys, there was a lot he didn't understand about females. It was a learning process for all of them. "When it's right to begin to see Susan again, could you let me know?" he asked.

Gradually God worked in all of their relationships, and when Susan and he did begin to see each other again, even her brother noticed a difference in how Jared treated her. A year and a half later Jared asked Susan to marry him, with Terry and Gil's blessing. Susan and Jared have now begun a lifelong marriage in which they bring out the best in each other and are growing in Christ.

COMMITTING TO GOD'S WILL

When we pray regarding our child's future and choice of a mate, as in every other prayer, it's important to want God's will more than our own, because this is a secret of true prayer. "Effectual prayer means being completely committed to God's will. The prayer that brings results—that is great in its power—is one where we don't give God the answers. We pray the needs up to God, and then we leave the decisions to Him. God is sovereign, and we must relax in His sovereignty, knowing that He knows best," says Evelyn Christenson.[1]

Your child or mine may be called to a life of singleness rather than marriage, and God's purpose might best be fulfilled in this way. That's why we must pray for God's leading and commit to His will rather than assume every person must marry.

We can always pray for good, close friendships and mentors—that God will bring people to strongly support, love, encourage, and work alongside our children in their calling and spiritual development. And that prayer may be answered through a marital partner or not. We can look at awesome people of God like Amy Carmichael and Patricia St. John to know that He will be faithful to provide all they need to carry out His purpose. Through their lives they can have many, even hundreds, of spiritual children. What's important is to let our children know that our love for them is strong and unconditional, whether they are married or single.

THE VALUE OF A THORN

Even when we pray for our children's mates and for their purity from the earliest ages, our prayers aren't always answered as we'd like. But God promises to be with us.

Kathy, a Tennessee mom, had always prayed for her daughter Nicole. But when Nicole was a sophomore at a Christian college, she made some poor choices and got pulled into a lifestyle she knew wasn't right. When she became pregnant, her mom's heart broke. Kathy had prayed for God to protect her children's virginity and for Him to guide her to a godly young man He designed for her, but that didn't happen.

Throughout Nicole's pregnancy, the Enemy brought many accusations to Kathy's mind: how God hadn't protected her daughter's virginity and how they'd failed as parents. Kathy had to rely on God's assurance that He gives our kids free will, just as He gave Adam and Eve—and each of us.

After much counseling, Nicole decided to keep her baby and come back home. Her parents were so thankful that their daughter never considered abortion. Yet many struggles remained.

Kathy and her husband had to work through their own anger…to forgiveness…to a real reconciliation. Although her plans for her daughter were shattered, she knows God is still sovereign, and He's always got a "Plan B." As Kathy's been held up in prayer by other mothers, so now she is able to encourage and pray for other hurting, discouraged moms. And she prays every day for her grandson, Jacob, that God will provide him an earthly daddy to love him as his own and love his mom as Christ loves the church. As God heals her, she holds on to a poem, which says:

Teach me the value of my thorn.
Show me that I have climbed to thee by the path of my pain.
Show me that my tears have made my rainbows.[2]

God promises to be with us, whether our children marry someone we would choose or not, whether our dreams for our children are fulfilled or disappointed. He says: "Do not fear, for I have redeemed you; I have called you by name; you are Mine! When you pass through the waters, I will be with you; and through the rivers, they will not overflow you. When you walk through the fire, you will not be scorched, nor will the flame burn you. For I am the LORD your God, the Holy One of Israel, your Savior... Do not fear, for I am with you" (Isaiah 43:1–5).

PUTTING FEET TO OUR PRAYERS

Few topics bring out that "Monster-Mother Thing"—or more tenacity and fervor in prayer—than this issue of "mates." Consider these specific guides for putting our hope in Him rather than in our own wisdom.

Give God your expectations. When we hang on to what we want and how we think God ought to work—our expectations—we become disappointed and anxious. But when we release our dreams and expectations for our children, we can rest in His sovereignty. Never stop praying, but trust in God's timing to direct their lives (or turn them around) instead of trying to make it happen on your schedule and terms. Remember all the times that He does so much more than we could ever ask or think (Ephesians 3:20). Commit to memory and pray these words often: "The Lord delights in those...who put their hope in his unfailing love" (Psalm 147:11, NIV).

Combine prayer with fasting. Jesus set the example for us to fast, not as a way to twist God's arm so that He blesses us or answers our prayers, but as a way to enter into a deeper intimacy with Him. If you want information on fasting, see the Recommended Reading list at the end of this book or Bill Bright's book *The Coming Revival: America's Call to Fast, Pray, and Seek God's Face.*

Follow the direction of Scripture. Scripture can lead you in praying for your children's future mate and their relationship. Consider praying the following passages:

- That they will be equally yoked (2 Corinthians 6:14)
- That they will love the Lord with all their heart, soul, mind, and strength and will build their home and relationship according to God's plan for marriage (Mark 12:29–30; Ephesians 5:20–25)
- That God will protect their purity, keep them from the wrong mate and save them for the right one, bringing them together in His perfect timing (2 Corinthians 6:14–17)
- That both will grow to spiritual maturity and will develop the wisdom needed to raise godly, wise children (Luke 2:51–52)
- That as they live together with Christ, their love will grow more perfect and complete (1 John 4:17)

Lord, You know the way my children should go;
lead them in Your everlasting way.
In their passage through life, in singleness or marriage,
grant that Your desires would become their desires,
and that You would be glorified in their lives.

In Christ's name. Amen.

Expect resistance

but

pray for miracles!

CORRIE TEN BOOM

CHAPTER TWELVE

THE FERVENT PRAYERS OF A GRANDMOTHER

For I am mindful of the sincere faith within you,
which first dwelt in your grandmother Lois, and your mother Eunice,
and I am sure that it is in you as well.
2 TIMOTHY 1:5

Florence Turnidge always prayed that her grandchildren would be caring and kind, that they would be lovers of God and people. And God gave her a chance to put feet to her prayers.

Florence had gone to the Crista nursing home near her house to visit Brother Everette, a Bible teacher, intercessor, and dear friend, who was confined to a wheelchair following a brain tumor. Even though she prayed with him and shared Scripture, he didn't recognize her or act as if he heard her. Walking home, she was so sad about his condition that she prayed aloud, "Lord, I'm not good around people who can't respond or speak. I'll go every week to visit Brother Everette, but it's going to be so hard. Please help me."

Just then she remembered how much he loved children. As soon as she reached her house, she called her daughter-in-law, Diane, and asked if she could take her granddaughter Jennifer to the nursing home the next time she went. Diane agreed, so on Thursday Florence walked to the home hand-in-hand with two-year-old Jennifer—her dark, curly-headed delight. Not knowing how her granddaughter would react, Florence explained on the way, "When we make people happy, we make Jesus happy."

As they walked up to Brother Everette, Florence said, "I brought Jennifer to see you. She's on the other side of your chair."

As he looked into the toddler's smiling face, framed by her long curls, his face broke into a smile.

Thus began many weekly visits, grandmother and granddaughter going to the nursing home. Now ten years later, Jennifer has a tremendous compassion for the elderly, and Florence has a thriving ministry. After Jennifer's positive response, Florence began taking her other grandchildren and neighborhood children to visit people at the nursing home. Currently she takes twenty-five children each month, ranging from babies to fifteen-year-olds.

"When we take the children in to sing, visit, and pray, it's like we've turned the lights on. They just make the place glow," says Florence. They have a great time, they bring great joy and life to the people in the home, and the children are developing into caring, compassionate people.

Florence is blessed by being close to her grandchildren, and she obviously makes a difference in their lives. Unfortunately, the majority of us don't have our children and grandchildren living nearby, but we can still make a positive difference in their lives, regardless of where they are. We can still be connected by prayer.

THE GRANDMOTHER HOT LINE

"In prayer, there is no generation gap. There is no distance at all, even if your grandchildren live a great distance away," says Deanna, an Oregon grandmother of six. The year Deanna had three grandchildren starting school she had to move several hours away. She'd been very active with her own children and wanted to be an involved grandparent.

As she prayed about her desire, she thought about her own grandmother, who had been a tremendous support in her life when she was growing up. They'd had a close relationship; in fact, in her junior high years when Deanna couldn't really talk to her mom, she shared the burdens on her heart with her grandmother. "Many times a granddaughter will talk with her grandmother because she's not giving advice. She's more inclined to listen and sympathize," says Deanna. How could she stay in touch and do for her grandchildren what had been done for her? The answer soon became clear: by praying for them.

Praying for our grandchildren grants us a special bonus. As we hold them up to the Lord in prayer, we draw closer to them and closer to Him as well. Praying for them is bonding. It strengthens our ties and gives them the very source of the strength of our own life—our relationship with the Lord. Standing in the gap for the grandchild you don't get to see often, you, like Deanna, can develop a heart-to-heart connection. In fact, your relationship can grow stronger.

Begin by letting your grandchildren know you're praying for them. Deanna does this by calling regularly and saying, "I'm praying for you. Do you have any specific requests, any problems I can pray about for you?" They love that she cares enough to ask and to pray for them.

At the beginning of the school year, she has each grandchild write a page that lists the names of their teachers and close friends, and subjects they really like and dislike. That gives her specifics to pray about. For instance, if they have a hard time in math, she makes certain she expressly prays for help in that area. This list goes into her prayer notebook.

With her younger grandchildren, she asks specific questions to find out what to pray for them. She'll ask about a teacher, as in, "I know this is your first year to have a male teacher. How are things going with Mr. Marshall?" When her granddaughter was eleven—and constantly bothered by a little boy at school—she would ask how William was doing. "William was always on our prayer list that year!" Deanna laughs.

Deanna took it a step further. Knowing the strength and support of praying with others, she gathered a group of grandmothers who, like her, wanted to stay in touch with God and their grandchildren. Some grandmothers agonized over their grandkids drifting into the wrong crowd or rebelling against their parents. Through prayer these grandmoms continue to provide help—the heavenly kind.

These grandmothers, ranging in age from fifty to eighty, make a notebook with a page for each grandchild that includes the child's photo and hand print. They meet every other week to lift up their grandchildren's needs and to thank God together for answering many prayers.

But their ministry extends beyond their family circles. Deanna encourages the other grandmoms to visit their grandchildren's schools if possible, as she does sometime during the year, and to send a note of encouragement to the teachers, telling how much they appreciate the teachers' efforts and that they're holding them up in prayer. Many schools host a "Grandparents' Day" when grandparents are invited to come to classes and eat lunch at school—a perfect opportunity.

JUST IN CASE YOU EVER DOUBT

One thing we know, when grandmothers pray, children's lives are impacted. Even if we die before we see the answers, our prayers aren't canceled when we go to heaven. They outlive us. A grandmother's prayer time is never in vain; it is time well invested in eternity.

First John 5:14–15 tell us, "And this is the confidence which we have before Him, that, if we ask anything according to His will, He hears us. And if we know that He hears us in whatever we ask, we know that we have the requests which we have asked from Him." That doesn't mean we'll always see the fruit of our prayers, but it does intimate that God takes our requests and works them out in His own way and timing.

Dennis Jernigan can testify to this. In the introduction to his song "I Long for the Day," he tells how his grandmother's prayers had a major influence on his life—but were answered years after her death. When he was a little boy, his grandmother often spoke to him about the Person of the Holy Spirit and told him words the Lord had shared with her. Dennis didn't always understand what she was talking about, but she imparted a sense of the eternal that stuck with him. When he was only twelve years old, his grandmother died—but not her influence.

As an adult Dennis became involved in the homosexual lifestyle before recommiting his life to Christ in his twenties. Then he applied his musical gifts as a pianist and songwriter to serving the Lord. At twenty-nine, Dennis took his worship team back to his hometown, Boynton, Oklahoma, to lead a community worship service.

After the worship service, his grandmother's prayer partner came to him and said, "Isn't it wonderful how your grandmother's prayers have been answered?"

In bewilderment and joy, Dennis asked, "What prayers?"

"Didn't you know?" she replied. "Your grandmother used to tell me how she would stand behind you as you practiced the piano at her house each day, and she would ask God to use you mightily in His kingdom to lead in music and worship. And He answered her prayers!"[1]

Dennis now serves all over the United States and the world, leading people of all ages and denominations and nations into worship. As he does, the effects of his grandmother's prayers not only touch his life but the lives of thousands.

WHEN WE CAN'T, GOD CAN

What about when your grandchild is having problems? When they hurt, or have unmet needs, or face difficult problems in their lives, we may not be able to fix the problems, but we can bring them to the God who can.

Catherine's grandson Jason always wanted to be a doctor, but just before he was to go to college, his father sustained a serious back injury and couldn't work any longer. Jason knew his parents wouldn't be able to provide him any money for college.

It broke Catherine's heart to see Jason's burning desire to be a doctor and his skills and intelligence to succeed, yet absolutely no money. She poured out her heart in prayer: "Oh, God, how can I help? I'm in no position to put Jason through college and medical school. I can give him a pittance but not enough to carry him."

Jason did attend college, by handling multiple jobs. He worked as a janitor and floor scrubber at the hospital and as an aide at a nursing home. He also worked as an emergency-room technician, eager to learn from everyone he could. Although Jason made excellent grades, he had to drop out of college one year to make enough money for the next. Instead of getting through college in four years, Jason spent six years, but he never complained or asked his family for money. As he persevered in his premed studies, his grandmother persevered in her prayers for him, sometimes even complaining to God about her inadequacy. "What can I do? We have thirteen other grandchildren. God, You'll have to help Jason; I can't."

By the time he graduated, Jason had made many friends in the medical profession. Doctors who had allowed him into the operating room observed his hard work and compassion toward the patients. When Jason applied and was accepted to Stanford Medical School, he received so many recommendations from high-ranking physicians and surgeons that he was awarded scholarships to take him all the way through his training.

When the good news came, Catherine was reminded of John 14:1: "Let not your heart be troubled; believe in God, believe also in Me." God had been preparing Jason all along, hearing and answering a grandmother's prayer.

COVERING YOUR GRANDBABY IN PRAYER

Maggie had loved being a mom and looked forward to being a grandmother someday. From the time her children were babies, she had prayed for them. Maggie's son Dave had always been close to his family and had plans to go to seminary, but when he fell in love with a young woman, those plans and family relationships derailed. She had a different lifestyle and didn't want anything to do with Dave's family—sisters, parents, or grandparents. As Maggie saw her son pulled farther and farther away, the strain grew between them.

Finally, Dave's wife made him choose between her and his family. Like a prodigal son, he left. For more than three years Maggie was excluded from his life. Dave went months without even speaking to his mom or dad. Maggie's heart was broken over losing her son. What if they had a baby? What if she never got to see her grandchildren?

"At times I couldn't even pray. It was like a death," she says. But Maggie kept asking God to cleanse her of resentment or any negative attitude and to show her how to pray for her son and daughter-in-law. One day when she was telling the Lord how much she missed her son, He impressed on her that Dave and his wife were going to have a baby. Maggie wrote it down in her journal and began to pray for her first grandchild.

For years she'd crocheted prayer blankets for new babies in her church, but why make one for this grandchild she might never see and who might not even be a reality? God nudged her to start one anyway. Sure enough, before long Maggie's son called to tell her they were expecting a child. Considering the due date, she later calculated that the baby was likely conceived the day God spoke to her. As Maggie crocheted the prayer blanket, she continued praying for her grandchild. Maggie gave the blanket to her daughter-in-law as a shower gift, along with the following letter:

> My precious one,
> In celebration of your arrival I've made you a special gift, called a prayer blanket. When you are covered with it, know that you are covered in prayer. Each tiny stitch represents a prayer prayed for you. Here are my ten prayers for you:
>
> 1. Like a ball of yarn that turns into a beautiful blanket, God has a beautiful plan for your life. I pray you discover it (Jeremiah 1:5).
> 2. This blanket is made with my human hands. But you are

"fearfully and wonderfully made" by divine hands. I pray you will know how special you are to God (Psalm 139:14).

3. If I miss a stitch, the blanket will unravel. God has wonderful plans for every step of your life. I pray you will look to Him for His plan and know that even when we as your family miss a stitch or make a mistake, God can redeem that as we trust Him (Proverbs 28:13).

4. If I go back and correct a stitch, the blanket won't be "holey." If you go back and confess your sins, your life will be holy. I pray you will have the courage to confess wrongdoing so you can live a holy life (1 John 1:9).

5. This blanket has many stitches, but they are nothing compared to the number of thoughts God has toward you. I pray you will think about God and know He thinks about you (Psalm 139:17).

6. It took three strands wrapped together to make a strong yarn for this blanket. It will take three parts (you, your family, and God) to make a strong life for you. And it will take three divine parts of God to keep you together. I pray you will depend on God and your family (Ecclesiastes 4:12).

7. The border on this blanket protects the blanket from becoming misshapen. God wants to put a border around your life to keep you safe from harm. I pray you will stay within the borders God sets for you (Job 1:10).

8. My hope for this prayer blanket is to keep you warm and secure. How much more is God's plan! He wants to give you a "future and hope." I pray you will always put your hope in God (Jeremiah 29:11).

9. When you are covered by this blanket, know you are covered in love and prayer. God wants to also cover you with the love of His Son. I pray you will come to love Jesus at an early age (John 14:21).

10. Although you will outgrow this blanket, I pray you will never want to outgrow your need for God (1 John 4:15–17).

Love,
Your grandmother

Since the baby's birth, the situation has begun to change between Maggie and her son and daughter-in-law; healing is gradually coming. Dave calls more now and recently asked his dad to spend a weekend with him out of town. Maggie was allowed to see her grandson, and when she held him for the first time, her first words to him were "Jesus loves you."

Maggie trusts God to continue what He has begun.

PUTTING FEET TO OUR PRAYERS

Whether you live next door to or are hundreds of miles away from your grandchildren, you can pray for them. Here are some reminders about ways you can bless them and influence their lives for Christ.

Write a letter and a Scripture prayer. To let her school-age grandchildren know she is praying for them, one grandmother writes the verse she's praying that week in calligraphy on a white card and then includes it in her letter to them.

Little reminders that you're praying can mean a lot to a child. When Jay, a young man with Down syndrome and a heart condition, was sick, his grandmother sent him a little "Pass It On" card. On it was a picture of an angel and Psalm 91:11: "For He will command his angels concerning you to guard you in all your ways" (NIV). She signed the back "Love and prayers, Grandmom." Months later Jay still puts it under his pillow every night and stands it up on his bedside table every day, as a tangible reminder of his grandmom's love and God's protection.

Start a Grandmothers In Touch group. How can you find other grandmothers to pray with weekly? First pray. Ask God to bring another grandmother to you. Also, pastors and women's ministry directors can point you to other grandmothers in their church who have a heart for prayer. Purchase the MITI book and request "Grandmothers In Touch" resources and a leader's guide for all the guidelines you need to lead the meetings.

Encourage each grandmom to make a simple prayer notebook with a page or two for each grandchild. Include information about the children, the school they're attending, the subjects they're studying, their teachers' names, and their hand prints and/or photos. Prayer requests and answers can be written on the page following. Using the notebooks in the meetings will help you stay focused, and recording the answers to your prayers will create a history of prayers for the family.

Let your grandchildren know you're praying for them. If you have a computer and modem, e-mail is a great way to share prayer requests. Asking for their prayer requests and then hearing how God works in their life keeps your hearts connected. Whether you are a grandmom, aunt, or great-grandmom, keeping in touch through prayer will make a tremendous difference—both now and in the years to come.

Lord, I will not conceal Your goodness
from my children or grandchildren
but with Your grace will tell the generation to come
the praises of the Lord. Help me to share with them
Your strength and the wondrous works You have done.

In Jesus' name. Amen.

ADAPTED FROM PSALM 78:4–7

Prayer has divided seas, rolled up flowing rivers,
made flinty rocks gush into fountains,
quenched flames of fire, muzzled lions, disarmed vipers and poisons,
marshaled the stars against the wicked,
stopped the course of the moon,
arrested the rapid sun in its great race,
burst open iron gates,
conquered the strongest devils,
commanded legions of angels down from heaven.
Prayer has bridled and changed the raging passions of man,
and routed and destroyed vast armies of proud, daring atheists.
Prayer has brought one man from the bottom of the sea,
and carried another in a chariot of fire to heaven;
what has prayer not done!

UNKNOWN

CHAPTER THIRTEEN

A Network of Love: Praying in Unity

If one member suffers,
all the members suffer with it;
if one member is honored,
all the members rejoice with it.
1 CORINTHIANS 12:26

We've seen what happens when a mother prays for her child and what happens when a group of women pray in agreement. Let's look at another level of prayer, where many people in different places join in praying for the same need. It's wonderful to pray with your spouse, prayer partner, or mothers group for some situations, but there are times when you need more prayer support. In fact, there are some circumstances so critical that you need an army of intercessors—a whole "intensive care unit " to pray. As E. M. Bounds said, "There is a cumulative effect in prayer. The focusing of many prayers on one life or on a situation can change defeat into victory."

Deidre, a New Zealand mother, experienced one of those times last year when her six-year-old son, Matthew, became gravely ill with meningococcal meningitis. As soon as she heard the doctor's diagnosis, Deidre called Ian, her husband, to join them and to phone their home group leader, asking for prayer. The leader immediately phoned others in the church to pray for Matthew. By this stage he was agitated, delirious, and unresponsive to his mom or the nurses. The dark spots on his body indicated he was in the advanced stage of meningitis, so the doctor ordered an ambulance and a resuscitation unit in case Matthew arrested en route to the hospital. The doctor had reason for alarm. Two kids in the area had recently died from the disease.

As soon as Deidre and Matthew arrived at the hospital, a woman approached Deidre, saying, "I know this is a terrible time for you, but I'm from TV-3, and we're doing a documentary about the children's hospital. Would you allow us to film what happens and your child's progress?"

Unconcerned about anything but her child's health, Deidre nodded yes and raced through the emergency-room doors. They were immediately led into the intensive care isolation room.

By this time, a network of people were earnestly interceding for Matthew—Deidre's Moms In Touch group, people in other churches, and those in his grandmother's church prayer chain.

Michelle, the ICU nurse on their case, informed Deidre and Ian what to expect. Matthew's face, legs, and arms would swell; he would likely be put on a respirator; and the spots would increase in size and turn black. For the next few hours Michelle stayed in the room, constantly watching Matthew's progress indicated by the barrage of monitors. A long, critical night lay ahead.

Despite being sedated, at one point in the middle of the night Matthew became so agitated that he fought the nurse who was attempting to get him to use a bedpan. So his mom sat him on her knee and rocked him. "The nurse came in again to see how things were, and he looked up at her with such wide, terrified eyes; it hurt me to the core to see his terror," says Deidre. "That's when I lost it. I just sat there rocking Matthew, tears pouring down my face. It was very difficult to pray. All I could do was weep and say, 'God, help.'"

By morning, Matthew was less distressed. Little by little they could see progress as his vital signs began to stabilize. When Michelle came back on duty, she read his charts, examined him, and said, "Well, Matthew, you must have had an angel looking down on you."

Matthew experienced none of the typical swelling. The massive headache the doctors predicted never came. The spots on his body began to slowly disappear. After being in ICU for twenty-four hours, Matthew was transferred to an isolation ward where he stayed for seven days, still a very sick little boy.

"I was very aware that many were praying; it felt like others were literally carrying me in their prayers. I felt the whole time like God was in control," Deidre said. Even having the TV crew filming them worked for their good in that Matthew received more medical attention.

But their big concern was how the meningitis would affect him long-term, since it can leave a child deaf or mentally handicapped. As the spots go black and cut off circulation, the aftereffects can be the loss of fingers, toes, a nose, or even ears. Yet Matthew had no long-term effects from the disease. He was on the mend, but God wasn't through yet.

The story of Matthew's recovery was used in a documentary which aired on national television throughout New Zealand. His grandmother, who was not a Christian, was truly awed by his healing and was drawn closer to God. Deidre's husband, Ian, who had never been a Christian or church attendee, was so touched by the outpouring of love and prayer for their son, the meals delivered daily, and the many ways people ministered to his family, he said he just had to go to church to "thank the people for their prayers."

Over the next few weeks the pastor built a relationship with Ian, and he started attending church more often. Ian came to a "Blue Moon Service" (especially geared for folks who come to church "once in a blue moon") and felt drawn to God. Before long, he went to the pastor after a service and made a commitment to Christ.

"Ian saw Jesus in the church folk. He saw God move and work mightily through prayer. He couldn't turn away from God anymore," says

Deidre. Through Matthew's illness, God brought him into a right relationship with Him. "Ian is still a baby in Christ," says Deidre, "and occasionally he takes a few steps backward, as we all do, but he is on the right road. Praise the Lord."

As R. A. Torrey says, "When we ask something definite of God, and He gives it, how real God becomes! He is right there! It is blessed to have a God who is real and not merely an idea.... The joy of the healing is not as great as the joy of meeting God."[1]

SHARING YOUR SPECIAL NEED

Sometimes we don't receive prayer support as Deidre's family did because people don't know about the problem or crisis we're experiencing. Some of us find it hard to ask others to pray, thinking the request may be a burden. Yet James 5:16 encourages us to "pray for one another." God knew we would need the prayer support of others. "There is a spiritual dynamic hinted at in the Bible that when two or more people prevail together in faith, praying in the spirit, their prayer power not only is added together, it seems multiplied."[2]

One mother came up with a simple and ingenious way to remind people to pray for her need. When Marilyn's youngest child was born with Down syndrome and had to have open-heart surgery a few months later to correct a birth defect, Marilyn wanted a way to remind people to pray for her daughter. So she made bookmarks with the baby's hospital photo on it and specific prayer requests underneath. After laminating the bookmarks, Marilyn and her husband gave them to their family, friends, members of their home fellowship group, and people at church who asked what they could do. Now they had a constant reminder of how they could help.

After the initial crisis passes, parents of a child with a special need often feel alone and unsupported. But not in Marilyn's case. A whole network of ongoing prayer support was created. People kept the prayer bookmark in their Bibles or devotional books so they remembered to pray for the baby in the months of recovery that followed her surgery. Marilyn's family felt the impact of the prayers, as they experienced being literally covered and carried by God's grace through many difficulties.

In our age of instant communication, a broad network of prayer support can be created almost immediately. When Jay, the son of my friend Louise, became ill and couldn't take a deep breath or even walk down the hall at the doctor's office, she was rightly worried. Jay had a congenital and progressive heart disease, so any infection was serious. As soon as the doctor said it could be pneumonia, Louise called her friend Pam on her cellular phone. Pam called the church secretary, who immediately posted the prayer request in the prayer room and notified the twelve pastors by e-mail and placed it on the church's web site. Pam and another friend called the special ministries team that Louise was part of. In less than thirty minutes over two dozen people were interceding for Jay.

Within those thirty minutes Jay's condition turned dramatically; it was like watching a miracle unfold. His color changed from extremely pale to normal. A trip to the hospital was averted, and even the doctor observed, "You look like a different kid than the one who came in here a short while ago!" United prayer makes a difference!

Our sense of privacy or our desire to be independent and self-sufficient should never prevent us or even make us hesitate to call for God's army and His weapons. Whether we are coping with an emergency or fighting an ongoing battle, God never intended for us to fight on our own. We not only receive blessings through others' prayers, we allow God to bless them by being part of His earthly task force.

RALLYING THE BODY

I love the way The Message expresses how God designed our bodies as a model for understanding how, as His church, our lives are part and parcel of each other, every part dependent on every other part. "If one part hurts, every other part is involved in the hurt, and in the healing" (1 Corinthians 12:26). Perhaps that healing comes from the compassion of Jesus—multiplied by the number of people identifying with the person's suffering and interceding for him—which releases God's love and power.

That love and power become like a lifesaver thrown to a drowning person. Judith Pitman, a British mother, experienced this when her teenage daughter, Annabel, had an undiagnosed illness which brought constant pain for over two months. Pain tablets helped very little, so Annabel couldn't lay, sit, or stand for any length of time, let alone sleep. Every night she half-sat and half-lay on her mom, and they dozed in between Annabel's bouts of severe pain.

Before long both mother and daughter were physically and spiritually drained. Because her teachers and fellow students showed no concern about her absence from school, Annabel also felt rejected and despondent. But Judith's Swiss MITI group and other Christian friends wrote notes, sent gifts, and made regular visits, restoring her confidence. Judith and Annabel also experienced intense moments of joy as they felt the prayers of these Christian friends. "We knew when the mothers were praying," says Judith, "for during the day a deep sense of God's love and comfort would envelope us. Each day someone inquired how Annabel was and asked for any prayer requests. Because of specific prayer on her behalf, we found a doctor who immediately diagnosed the illness as a virus in her spinal cord."

Eighteen months have passed since the onset of her illness. She is still recovering, and they are still seeing wonderful answers to prayer. When Annabel had to repeat the third year of high school, she was placed in a class with concerned and sympathetic teachers and classmates. Since then she has blossomed and is making good grades.

Judith says, "Looking back, I'm not sure how I would have coped without my 'prayer line.' We pray in the confidentiality and security of knowing we are true sisters in the Lord."

MULTIPLIED POWER

What happens when the network of prayer support extends even farther? What does God do in the lives of the people receiving the prayer support and the lives of those who are praying? When the Body of Christ unites with a central focus—when mothers groups, congregations, prayer chains, and individuals cry out to God with a common prayer—He seems to be glorified in special ways, and His power becomes more apparent to both believers and unbelievers.

"When many people unite in prayer, spiritual power is multiplied," says Wesley Duewel. "As you pray together, the prayer of each helps deepen the hunger for God's answer and helps fan into flame the spirit of prayer. Faith for God's answer is strengthened, and all those who unite in prayer begin to sense God's power in a new way."[3] At the same time, a network of love is formed that surrounds the person in crisis—and his or her family—deeply touching each of their lives.

When an illness threatened the life of a Beeville, Texas, college student, she and her family didn't battle it alone; a whole city, her college campus, the churches in Abilene, Christians in Dallas where she was hospitalized, and hundreds of people she'd never met hurt with her and rallied in prayer. And in so doing, lives were changed. People who hadn't attended church in years came back and renewed their relationship with God, and the lives of Cameron and her mother were remarkably touched.

Following the end of her freshman year of college, Cameron went into the hospital to have a lump removed from her thyroid and biopsied. Simple procedure, the doctors had said. They expected her to be in the hospital two days at the most. When the lump was found to be malignant, however, they took her back into surgery to remove her entire thyroid gland to make certain it didn't spread. The diagnosis was ominous—malignant follicular cancer—but the doctors assured her parents they had taken care of it.

Then Cameron's neck ballooned to twice its normal size, as air was leaking out of her trachea. The swelling cut off her breathing, and she was rushed into emergency surgery.

Next, her blood pressure dropped severely as toxic shock syndrome set in, causing hallucinations. Back in emergency surgery once again, doctors were shocked to find a deadly flesh-eating bacteria the size of a quarter in her neck. After cleaning it out, a powerful antibiotic was administered. By then the bacteria had eaten through three rings of her windpipe, so Cameron couldn't get enough air. She was again taken into surgery, this time for an emergency tracheostomy.

As a team of twenty specialists was called in to consult on Cameron's case, the Holy Spirit conducted an orchestra of prayer. Many of the twenty-five thousand people in Cameron's hometown were interceding for her, including people from eighteen different churches. They put Cameron on their prayer chains and in their Sunday bulletins every week. Hundreds of cards with written prayers and Scriptures flooded in. One of her professors at Abilene Christian University called not only the whole campus but twenty-five other congregations in the city to pray for Cameron. For six and a half weeks, her life hung in the balance as she endured seventeen major surgeries and forty-three surgical procedures. "It was like being in the eye of a hurricane," says her mother, Gayle. "I cried every time she went into surgery." Cameron lost thirty pounds and most of her hair. All of her veins collapsed, and a central line had to be inserted in her neck. She developed pneumonia and a lung collapsed. She had seizures from a medication. The flesh-eating bacteria spread to her heart sac and lungs. Then a delicate experimental surgery had to be performed to insert a flap on her neck because the tracheal hole wasn't healing.

One night Cameron felt she was dying, drowning in her own blood. At this critical moment, the church members back in Beeville were in the parking lot, leaving the evening service. All of a sudden, someone got word that Cameron was going in for yet another emergency surgery. Everyone filed back into the church to pray in one accord for healing. Doctors were able to stop the bleeding that night, but more complications developed. Her church, community, and family continued praying for her; in fact, the worse she got, the more people heard of her condition and prayed, including many strangers.

Many days, forty or fifty people from Dallas churches who had heard about Cameron would be in the waiting room, praying for her during surgery. When one doctor came out of the operating room to inform her parents of her condition, he saw the crowd and said, "I didn't know I was going to have a congregation to talk to!"

Although she and her family will never know how many prayers were laid at the feet of God on her behalf, she can count the more than two thousand letters they received, many from people they didn't even know were praying. One from a friend of her mother's hundreds of miles away read, "Every day I lift your name to God. Do you suppose God ever says, 'Here comes another prayer for Cameron Manskur' and smiles? I'll bet He does!"

Defying all medical expectations, Cameron survived this nightmare—and another cancer scare the following year. How does she view her terrifying experience? There is no bitterness about "Why did this happen to me?" Instead, she wrote in her journal in the midst of her battle, "We must all pray as much as possible to God, because He will answer. I've put all my faith in Him that He will heal me and that He can fight off the devil or whatever it is that has tried to take over. I will, along with You, God, beat this. I promise."

Now back at college, she's stronger in her faith—and absolutely certain of the power of prayer.

PUTTING FEET TO OUR PRAYERS

Consider the following ideas about developing networks of prayer.

Start a prayer chain. If your church doesn't have an active prayer chain, start one. Then in case of emergencies and severe illness, a network of caring intercessors can be quickly mobilized to pray. One such chain, called "Prayer Band," begins in Virginia. Ruth, the leader, makes seven long-distance and four local calls. Within approximately ten minutes, three hundred intercessors in thirty-six churches are praying throughout the Tidewater area, Washington, D.C., and North Carolina.

Whether it is a heart attack, a runaway teenager, or a child bitten by a rattlesnake, the prayer chain covers the situation in united prayer. They are seeing marvelous answers as God intervenes in healing and salvation. Some of the churches follow up by putting the prayer needs in their bulletin each Sunday. "We try to impress on people that it is for emergencies, and we ask for a volunteer prayer leader in each church," says Ruth. You can develop your own guidelines, such as the type of requests to be put on the prayer chain.

In case of an emergency, you could serve as a contact person for family members. You could check daily on needs and then call prayer requests to those who will faithfully intercede.

Remember that God isn't limited by the size of our army. We need to have a balanced understanding about prayer. Although at times like these just described many intercessors are needed, God's intervention in a situation isn't limited by our resources or dependent upon our numbers. Look at what He did with David, the shepherd boy who single-handedly faced Goliath armed only with a slingshot. Look at how the Midianites were defeated by Gideon's small army that followed God's direction. (Read Judges 7 for the inspiring story.)

Whether we are by ourselves, with a friend or a group of mothers, or part of a large prayer effort, what matters is that we seek God. And He, the God of all Hope, will hear us and act!

Lord, grant that when others in my church,
neighborhood, or circle of friends
suffer, You would fill my heart with compassion,
and Your love would motivate me to faithfully intercede for them.
Make me part of Your network of love on the earth.

In His name. Amen.

FOR OUR CHILDREN

Father, hear us, we are praying,
Hear the words our hearts are saying,
We are praying for our children.

Keep them from the powers of evil,
From the secret, hidden peril,
From the whirlpool that would suck them,
From the treacherous quicksand, pluck them.

From the worldling's hollow gladness
From the sting of faithless sadness
Holy Father, save our children

Through life's troubled waters steer them,
Through life's bitter battle cheer them,
Father, Father, be Thou near them.

Read the language of our longing,
Read the wordless pleadings thronging,
Holy Father, for our children.

And wherever they may bide,
Lead them Home at eventide.

AMY CARMICHAEL

CHAPTER FOURTEEN

PRAYERS THAT GO AROUND THE WORLD

"Who can say but that God
has brought you into the palace
for such a time as this?"

ESTHER 4:14, TLB

One thing I have discovered in the process of interviewing women all over the world is that despite our different races, religions, and nations, our mother hearts are alike: They beat for our children. Just as Christian moms in America are concerned about secular curriculum, Christian mothers in a Muslim country cry because their children are taught about Islam in school. Moms in Switzerland and New Zealand worry about the New Age influence in their children's textbooks just as mothers in America do. Moms in Tanzania and Brazil are concerned about drugs and alcohol just as we are. Mothers all over the world worry about their children's safety.

Everywhere, mothers' hearts break when prodigal teens love the world instead of God's ways, when they get into bad relationships or make wrong choices, when they're lonely and have no friends. We all long for our children's emotional, physical, and spiritual well-being; we want them to love God with all their hearts and minds. Mothers want their children to do well in school; for many, it's the only escape from poverty. We see the bright spark in our kids and desperately want them to learn, develop their gifts, and reach their God-given potential.

Mothers around the world recognize they can't control all the forces that threaten their children's well-being. They feel helpless when their kids are hurt or sick, and they have a great need for the support of others in carrying the burdens they feel for their children.

Yet there are also some major differences in mothers' experiences. Whereas we in America have almost unlimited freedom to meet to support each other in prayer and in studying the Bible together, believers in many countries are persecuted for any Christian activities, including prayer. In China, Sudan, and Ethiopia, along with many Middle Eastern countries, people are still imprisoned and killed for their faith. In some of those countries, women risk their very lives just to get together with other believers to pray.

From time to time we must raise our eyes to the horizon and see that the world is much bigger than our own personal needs, our family and community. There are many needs in other parts of the world, and God is answering the prayers of those mothers as well. We have much we can learn from these prayers...that go around the world.

PRAYERS THAT BRING HOPE

When the school year was about to start, a group of Christian mothers in a Middle Eastern country[1] were feeling desperate. Their country is in crisis, as are many in that region, and believers are suffering persecution. Muslim extremist groups, fueled by the same forces that have ripped apart Iraq, have increased in fierceness, causing terror to escalate.

"We were in a state of despair," one of these women wrote. "We felt that as mothers we had surrendered to the enemy, letting him steal our children. Our schools do not know nor teach a thing about the Lord Christ. Yet we must send them to school. And there are no free Christian schools to teach our children.... We thought that we were not capable of doing anything.... We mothers have stood handcuffed."

But God heard their cries, and a week after the school year started, a missionary put a little white booklet into this mother's hands, a booklet with "Moms In Touch" written in Arabic across the front. This mom said, "When I looked at the title, I laughed in my heart, saying, 'How could a Western woman understand and feel what an Eastern woman suffers?'"

But she hadn't finished the introduction before she realized that their problems were similar. As she says, "Satan is in every place, fighting our children, although with different strategies from one country to another. The result is the same: to snatch our children as prey in his hands. But thanks be to God who leads us in His triumph and who led someone to share this vision of prayer with our people too."

The MITI booklet she had received had been translated into Arabic by a native woman in the early 1990s and was later finished by an American missionary. When the first two hundred booklets were snatched up and distributed by pastors, he saw how desperately the women needed these prayer groups. He then found a way to get twenty-three thousand of the booklets printed and distributed, even though any unapproved printing of Christian materials could result in imprisonment.

That's why this little booklet was received with such joy. It was the first Christian book ever published in Arabic just for women. A letter from a new MITI group explains: "We believe that the Lord, who has sent you for such a time as this, must have spoken to you to distribute the book this week in particular, which is such a wonderful act, and which has amazed us...." It came the very week school was starting, and the mothers were crying out to God in despair over their children and the condition of the schools. Now their hopelessness and handcuffs were broken, for there was something important they could do on their children's behalf.

SHARING THE VISION

These mothers started praying and sharing the vision with other women, and in the first year nearly thirty groups of mothers began praying together for their children and for the schools. Every major city and many towns now have a Moms In Touch weekly gathering. Some Coptic (Orthodox) mothers were drawn into the groups by their desire to pray for their children. Then, in the process of participating in the praise, the thanksgiving, and intercession, they met Jesus! Many have made commitments to Christ and had their lives and families transformed.

The mother who volunteered to train and coordinate the prayer groups in this country was pressured by the government to curb her ministry activities. Her husband was removed from his job and given another job, requiring a two-hour commute, to minimize his ministry activities and to serve as a warning.

When she had to step down, another woman felt the Lord's call to take her place. Miraculously, she got a visa to go to California for the 1994 Moms In Touch Tenth Anniversary Celebration. It was the first time she had ever been out of the country or spent a night away from her children and husband. She returned home with an even greater zeal for this ministry.

Then suddenly, persecution of the believers increased. All Christian activity was shut down. No meetings were allowed anywhere except in registered churches, and these were bombed or burned regularly by terrorist groups. A curfew was established due to increased violence at night. Many believers were killed. Young girls were raped, and mothers feared less for their own lives than for their daughters' safety. Meanwhile, the prayer booklets quietly circulated among the mothers and grandmothers, showing them how to cover their children in prayer.

"Their faith is so strong," said an American liaison. "'To live is Christ, to die is gain' is a reality to them. But they fear for their children."

Even two or three women gathering in a home aroused suspicion, especially if they were known to be Christians. So the ministry had to either stop or go underground. The moms who did meet to pray or to get training to lead a group did so at their own peril. Truly, for them the ministry was a life-and-death matter.

During the time of harassment and persecution, the coordinator experienced great discouragement and heaviness. She was threatened with losing her job if she carried on any ministry activities. But her American sisters in MITI kept praying for her and the other mothers in her country. They prayed that although the ministry couldn't be active now God would continue preparing her for the time when the doors did open and she could continue.

Even when they couldn't meet together, these women held on to their hope—hope that their prayers would make a difference for their children, hope in the promises of God's Word for their daughters' protection and their sons' deliverance, hope that God really cared for them and had heard their cries, hope that their children would be strong in their faith and not be influenced by Islam, and hope to make a place for themselves in society and God's kingdom.

"Once we were hopeless, but we are no longer," wrote the MITI leader. "Now we know what we should do for the sake of our children and the schools. How we thank the Lord Jesus Christ...for your faithfulness because you didn't keep this vision to yourself, nor to America only."

Throughout the three years of persecution, they looked forward to the day they might meet again and pray. From the outside, it appeared the groups were gone and the ministry stalled. Then the tide turned. Some of the pressure has lifted, and the mothers have boldly begun to meet in small groups to pray—still cautiously, but joyfully. The vision for mothers praying is stronger than ever.

As one mother said, "We have gone through an exceedingly difficult situation. During this time, we were not able to continue our work because of the outside pressure that affected our hearts and souls. But we did not despair. Diligently we continued in prayer day and night, asking the Lord to intervene and to give us the way out. And sure enough, we have started our meetings again. This is because of the many prayers lifted up both within and without."

Revival in this country and throughout the Middle East is growing with the same intensity as the opposition, says a woman involved in ministry to the country. "Muslims are receiving Christ at an unprecedented rate, with miracles of healing and deliverance. The Lord is hearing and answering the prayers of His people, and the blood of the martyrs is giving rise to an even greater revival as the walls of Islam come down. How gracious is our God, that He should allow us to have played a part in helping our sisters learn how to pray for the children whom God is raising up for Himself."

In Brazil, thousands of moms are praying their children into the kingdom and onto the mission field. Founder Ana Maria Pereira has gathered women from every social class and region of Brazil who sign a commitment to pray fifteen minutes each day that their children would come to Christ and go to those who have never heard the gospel. The praying moms meet every month in local churches to pray and share testimonies of God's power that has changed their kids' lives and how fervent prayer has turned kids from destruction or drugs to follow Christ. "Wake Up Deborah," as this prayer movement is called, is spreading from Brazil to other nations and is literally changing the face of missions.

When I hear from Middle Eastern mothers or Brazilian mothers, I'm so strongly reminded that nothing is impossible for God....

When I read letters from Middle Eastern mothers, I'm so strongly reminded that nothing is impossible for God. "When we are facing the impossible, we can count on the God of the Impossible," said Amy Carmichael.[2] Is there anything in your life that seems impossible? Maybe having a disciplined prayer life—given the demands on your time. Perhaps an overwhelming burden that you feel is "unfixable." Just as God has brought these mothers in the Middle Eastern country through despair and persecution into hope, He can bring you a new beginning.

PUTTING FEET TO OUR PRAYERS

Here are some practical ways to broaden the horizon for your prayers.

Adopt a country. As you read about these mothers in the Middle East, did your heart go out to them? Let the Lord expand your heart beyond your personal concerns as you pray for one of these countries where groups of mothers are meeting weekly, sometimes at their own peril: Romania, Russia, Egypt, South Korea, Indonesia, Egypt, Nigeria, Mexico, Africa, Greece, China, and Taiwan. If praying for the world sounds too huge, ask God to give you one prayer assignment, a specific country or burden for which you can intercede.

Pray for moms groups. Pray that there will be a group of praying mothers for every school—public and private—in cities and towns worldwide. Satan hates prayer, so he throws obstacles in our way no matter where we are. In South Africa, for example, moms are concerned about Satanism, rampant drug use, lack of discipline in schools, overcrowded classes, and, like us, lack of time. "Everybody says they are too busy, rushing children everywhere, moms working. They find it difficult to find space in their schedules to meet and pray. But we are definitely not giving in," says Rosemary, the South Africa MITI coordinator.

Pray that moms everywhere will catch the vision and experience firsthand that being with one other mom before the Lord will free them from feeling hopeless. Pray that mothers who are interceding will be confident that they are making a difference in children's lives!

Oh, Lord, be with the precious mothers in other countries
who have so little, yet love You so much.
Strengthen their hearts. Put a hedge of protection around them,
and remind us to pray for them.
Give these mothers hope and a strong commitment to pray
for their children and schools. And raise up moms in every nation
to lead the way in prayer.
For Christ's sake. Amen.

Prayer constantly enlarges our horizon and our person.
It draws us out of the narrow limits
with which our habits, our past,
and our whole personage confine us.
PAUL TOURNIER

CHAPTER FIFTEEN

WHEN GOD ASKS US TO PUT FEET TO OUR PRAYERS

"Enlarge the place of your tent;
Stretch out the curtains of your dwellings,
spare not; lengthen your cords,
and strengthen your pegs.
For you will spread abroad
to the right and to the left."

ISAIAH 54:2–3

As I reflect on my prayer journey, I'm more aware than ever how God uses our personal concerns to enlarge our hearts and pass on His blessings to others. The concern we felt for our son when he was battling asthma caused my husband and me to study more diligently what the Bible says about prayer and healing. As we learned to pray more effectively for him, we had more compassion for others. That led to our joining the Servants in Prayer ministry in our church, where over a period of years we prayed for many people, both in the hospital and in prayer services. It also led to Holmes going on a prayer mission to Taiwan with others from our church. With each step, God broadened our perspective and moved us to action.

God uses our personal experiences to develop this "wideness of heart," this reaching out to others, much as 2 Corinthians 1:3–4 describes: "The

Father of mercies and God of all comfort...comforts us in all our affliction so that we may be able to comfort those who are in any affliction with the comfort with which we ourselves are comforted by God." In comforting others by praying for them, we pass on what God has graciously given us.

This passing on of comfort happens over and over again when two mothers start meeting regularly to pray for their children and then are so blessed that they share it with others. That's how the ministry of praying moms has gone all over the United States and Canada and into many countries throughout the world—from one woman telling another and then another what a big difference prayer makes in her life, and widening her circle of care.

GOING BEYOND OUR COMFORT ZONES

In the process, God has gently nudged women out of their comfort zones and into ministry and leadership. Often He seems to choose a quiet woman, one who prefers the background, to gather women and lead them in a prayer group. Isabella was so shy she would ask others to pray. She says, "When I had a burden, I always felt other people could use the right words better than I could and God would answer my problem better." But through a small prayer group of mothers in Scotland, her whole view of prayer changed; she learned that God did indeed hear her and would answer her prayers. So when she moved to England, she reached out to women in her town and started a Moms In Touch group.

Women who have relocated because of their husband's jobs or ministries have been a primary force behind scattering seeds of prayer internationally. When Ingrid lived with her family in Egypt, she began praying with a Moms In Touch group that interceded weekly for a German school. She had experienced how prayers could calm their anxieties and concerns for their children and could change the schools and their kids' lives. So when she moved to Germany, she took her vision for praying moms with her. "I caught the American idea in Egypt and then brought it to Germany!" Ingrid says. "It is good for the mothers to start to believe that the promises in the Bible are for us today so we can put them into practice."

Ingrid started putting the promises into practice in her "Mutter in Kontakt" group with women of different nationalities—Czechoslovakian, Rumanian, Lebanese, German, and Korean—as they prayed weekly for their children. All Ingrid had for her group was an English Moms In Touch booklet, and it was soon evident that a German translation was needed. Since she is Swedish and her husband is Swiss, she looked for someone to translate the book, but God kept pointing to her to do the job. Writing the German version was definitely out of her comfort zone, but Ingrid stepped out in faith, started the translation, and found some German women to edit the booklet. After her careful work and the financial help of the American MITI, the German translation was completed, printed, and distributed in both Germany and Switzerland.

MATCHING THE WALK WITH THE TALK

Be prepared. What you pray for, God may ask you to take part in effecting. An Oregon mom who calls herself "The Reluctant Ambassador" learned this firsthand. Several years ago Barbara Hicks, an Oregon MITI area coordinator, began praying for and financially supporting two pastors in Africa—one in Tanzania and one in Uganda. As she prayed for people to come to know Christ through these pastors' crusades, she developed a great burden for the countries. Later as she was wondering how to spread the word about Moms In Touch, she thought of sending one MITI booklet to each pastor. "Such a simple thing to do—to send those prayer booklets," she says. "I hadn't a clue that hundreds of women would join Moms In Touch as these pastors spread the word in crusades all around their countries." She also had no idea that *her* life would be affected in a powerful way.

To facilitate sharing this idea of moms praying, one of the pastors translated the MITI booklet into Swahili and gave the first copy to Diana

Mushi, a Tanzanian mother. Diana immediately caught the vision of MITI and helped start groups in numerous churches.

At the same time a team of people from Barbara's church were planning a trip to Africa and invited her to go along to share with women about prayer. But Barbara had no desire to go to Africa. That was totally out of her comfort zone! "I agonized for two weeks trying to hear God's will. I wanted to talk to women about Moms In Touch, but I'm not a 'speaker.' Nor did I want to get a tropical disease, sleep on the floor, take a bath with only a cup of water, be hot, leave my family for a month, be right next to Rwanda, ride on an airplane for twenty-three hours (twice!), suffer jet lag, give up electricity, or sleep under a mosquito net," she says.

But as Barbara prayed, God transformed her reluctance to obedience, and she agreed to go. With many mothers praying for her, Barbara flew with a team to Tanzania and spoke five different times to about a hundred African ladies each time, encouraging them to pray for their children and schools. She was amazed at how many groups had already started with just one booklet in each country.

But not everyone was glad for their presence. Before their team went to one city, a school was bombed to prevent their coming, killing eight children and injuring eighty others. After a church in Uganda prayed all night, four Muslims were caught the next day planting a bomb in the place where they were to meet next. While the whole team mourned the tragedy and were frightened by the news, they also felt covered by the many prayers for their safety.

The trip held blessings and surprises. Barbara had never experienced joy as she did worshiping with African Christians in their three-hour church services. Even though they sat on wooden benches without backs, in a building with stick walls, a dirt floor, and a thatched roof, she hardly noticed. "The praise was so exciting, the service so honoring to God, that even when hard rains came and made rivers under our benches, we just moved our feet and let the rivers go!"

There were many specific answers to prayer. Barbara didn't get malaria, and God healed a severe pain in her hip and leg. The whole team was kept safe. And hundreds of women in Tanzania were encouraged to pray for their children. As a result, God is answering the prayers of mothers in Africa for the specific problems they and their children face.

One of the biggest struggles women in Tanzania face is "broken houses" or broken families. Families are coming apart. Diana Mushi's group has so many needs that they meet two times a week: Wednesdays to pray for their children and schools, and Fridays to pray for their husbands, marriages, church, and nation.

One of the mothers had been separated from her husband for three years after he left her for another woman. The moms cried before God on this family's behalf. "In May of this year, we all celebrated the renewed wedding!" says Diana.

Another mother in their group was married to a Muslim with four Muslim children. After the group prayed for this family for one year, God touched the father and children, and they became Christians.

Young people they have prayed for have been delivered from drug abuse, and several children have been physically healed.

"It's true that we're ordinary weak human beings, but we don't use human plans and methods to win our battles. Prayer is our weapon and our strength comes from our Lord," says Diana.

As a result of God's grace, over four hundred mothers are now praying for the children and schools in Dar es Salaam, Mwanza, Mbeya, Moshi, and Arusha. "There is revival starting in my country; please pray for us!" says Diana.

A CHALLENGE CLOSE AT HAND

God doesn't have to take us out of the country to take us out of our comfort zones. You might find God challenging you, as he did Valerie Eaton, to go way beyond your comfort zone without ever leaving your state.

Valerie, an Oregon mom, had led a prayer group for her children's school, but when Fran, a woman with a ministry to incarcerated women, asked her to come to Salem Penitentiary to share about prayer, she was nervous. She sensed God was giving her an opportunity to pass on what He'd given her, so despite feeling uncomfortable, she prayed for God's help and for His heart of love toward these moms.

Mothers, grandmothers, and aunts gathered around her at a table. And Valerie soon realized that these mothers who are behind bars carry burdens for their children just as other moms do, but have less chance to nurture them and provide for their needs. Some worry about their children's living situations while they are in prison. They agonize over not being able to tuck their kids in bed, provide clothes and school supplies, or offer a listening ear. Some don't get to see their kids because the children live too far away to visit them. One woman who was only eighteen was to deliver her baby in a week and then have to give her up. These women are handcuffed, virtually helpless to do anything for their children.

As Valerie walked them through the Four Steps of Prayer, she prayed a scripture for each of their children, reading it aloud with them and putting in their child's name. One by one tears began to flow down their faces as their eyes were opened—this was something they could do for their children!

"You may not be able to take your children on your lap and provide the things they need," Valerie told them. "But even here in prison you have the ability to pray for your child—and that's the most important thing you can do." Perhaps for the first time in many years, these women had hope that they could positively influence their children's lives.

By Valerie stepping out and ministering to those in prison—one of the special groups Jesus mentions in Matthew 25, and one of the most overlooked—women in Salem Penitentiary began to meet to intercede for their children.

PRAYER IN ACTION

I find prayer often leads us to action. In fact, prayer *is* action. And in a sense, all our actions are prayers; our whole life is a prayer for good or evil.[1] But we can be assured that when God calls us to action, His grace will sustain us, and He will do exceedingly above all that we think or ask.

I love what Fern Nichols shared with me about walking in simple, daily obedience: "On any given day, when the Lord tells you to do something, just be obedient. You don't know what He's going to do with that obedience. The Lord is the one who works in and through us to accomplish His purpose. Each day it's our small obedience, and He will do the grand thing."

PUTTING FEET TO OUR PRAYERS

What step might God be asking you to take to put your prayers into action? You might consider the following ideas to find out.

Pray for God to stretch you. What need or concern do you feel passionately about? What country do you have a burden for? What breaks your heart? As you pray about it, be willing to be part of the answer—to join your prayers with action if God so leads you.

It might mean gathering a few mothers in your neighborhood or school to pray with you, even if you are one of those quiet women who doesn't consider herself a "leader." If God has a plan for you, He'll equip you. It might mean starting a prayer group in a women's prison, praying for and tutoring an inner-city child, or mentoring and discipling a young single mother. It might even mean encouraging women in another country to pray for their children and schools.

"The great thing is to give what has strengthened and kindled your own soul. Then it is sure to kindle others," said Amy Carmichael.[2] Second Timothy 2:2 says it well: Take what you have and pass it on to others.

How can you pass on to someone else the blessings you've received from God in prayer?

Pray for the country coordinators. Pray for the coordinators of prayer groups in countries throughout the world. In New Zealand alone, Deidre Chicken coordinates over three hundred groups out of a little home office while caring for her three children and husband and holding down a job. They are seeing much fruit from their prayers. In Tanzania, Diana Mushi encourages mothers and coordinates MITI groups without office equipment or space. These moms need help, funds for equipment and office space, and our prayers. Ask God to use you in helping them carry out what He has called them to do.

Lord, we pray that You will lead us to put our prayers into action.
We pray for You to send us as laborers into these prisons of darkness,
whether they be physical or political or spiritual.
Use each of us to do our part, in our neighborhoods
or across the world, to cover our children in prayer.
Make us faithful in prayer, and grant us courage
and obedient hearts to take action when You lead.

In Jesus' name. Amen.

More things are wrought by prayer
Than this world dreams of.
Wherefore let thy voice
Rise like a fountain for me day and night.

ALFRED LORD TENNYSON

CHAPTER SIXTEEN

THE FOOTPRINTS OF PRAYERS

The prayer of a person living right with God
is something powerful to be reckoned with.
JAMES 5:16, THE MESSAGE

Have you ever heard of Mary Ball, Elizabeth Newton, or Ni Kwei-tseng? Perhaps not, but I'll bet you've heard of their children—George Washington, John Newton, and Madame Chiang Kai-shek.

Mary and Elizabeth and Ni were women with a big vision, and their stories show what far-reaching effects prayers can have, far beyond the span of the pray-er's life. Viewing these "stories behind the stories" from the perspective of many years later, we can truly see the footprints left by these women's prayers and be encouraged that just as surely as God worked through their prayers, He will act in our children's lives through our prayers.

THE BULLETPROOF PRESIDENT

George Washington, first president of the United States, was the son of Mary Ball Washington, a somewhat nervous and overprotective mother.

When at twenty-one years old Washington was invited to become General Braddock's aide during the French and Indian wars, his mother strongly protested. After all, he was young and had much potential, and he was her son! She had already refused his request to join the British Royal Navy when he was merely fourteen. He had worked as a surveyor instead, but by the time he was twenty, he was serving in the Virginia Militia. Although he had no training or experience, he was soon commissioned as a major. No wonder his mother worried.

"Concerned for his safety, she hurried to Mount Vernon to persuade him not to accept the invitation but was unable to discourage him. In their conversation, he reminded her: 'The God to whom you commended me, madam, when I set out upon a more perilous errand, defended me from all harm, and I trust he will do so now. Do not you?'"[1] Doesn't that sound like an adventurous young man who loved the military and thought his mom was being overprotective (and knew how to work her!)?

Before he left, however, it is said that he knelt before his mother's rocking chair while she prayed for God's protection on his life. Washington later credited his mother's prayers[2] for his surviving many crises and several massacres in the British campaigns that followed. In one incident, General Braddock lay dead along with hundreds of the Virginia troops, yet Washington wasn't even wounded. In later battles Indian marksmen and chiefs told of shooting at Washington numerous times without killing him.[3]

How did Washington explain it? He wrote to his brother after the Fort Cumberland massacre, "By the all-powerful dispensation of Providence, I have been protected beyond all human probability or expectation; for I had four bullets through my coat, and two horses shot under me, yet escaped unhurt, although death was leveling my companions on every side of me!"[4]

A SLAVE TRADER TURNED MINISTER

As Elizabeth Newton walked home from the Dissenter's Chapel with her little son, John, she dreamed he would some day be a minister like their pastors, Isaac Watts and David Jennings. Although her husband attended the Church of England, he was a ship captain and was at sea for months at a time, so Elizabeth had the primary influence on her son's early life. Elizabeth taught young John not only reading, writing, and math but also catechism and the Bible. A godly, tender mother, she prayed earnestly with and for her son.

However, before John's seventh birthday, his young mother died of tuberculosis, and he was left in the care of his stepmother and his mostly absent father, who provided almost no spiritual influence or nurture. Captain Newton had a different view of his son's future than Elizabeth had had—and so John took his first sea voyage at age eleven.

Through his teens and twenties, John's moral and spiritual life spiraled downward. In his effort to run away from God, this prodigal indulged in all kinds of debauchery and cruelty, repeatedly blasphemed God's name, and attempted to take as many as possible to hell with him. John became a slave trader and narrowly escaped death numerous times. For over a year he even was held as a slave himself in Africa, where he almost starved to death.

After twenty-two years of rebellion against God, John Newton found himself one night in a raging storm at sea—a storm so violent that he had himself tied to the helm in order to steer the ship. In those desperate eleven hours, Newton cried out to God and found himself recalling prayers from childhood, his mother's words, the teachings of the catechism, and scriptures. He "grasped at God's outstretched hand" and was saved by His amazing grace.[5]

This began Newton's transformation. By the age of thirty-eight, he was ordained a minister in the Church of England, where he served God as a parish pastor, evangelist, and hymn writer. He helped bring the evils of the slave trade to light and had a profound impact on William Wilberforce, whose influence in Parliament led to the abolition of slave trade in the British Empire. Although Newton founded missionary and Bible societies worldwide and brought many to Christ through his preaching, his greatest gift may have been writing "Amazing Grace."

Who paved the way for God's amazing grace to redeem this "wretch"?

"His mother's prayers had prevailed in spite of all Satan's efforts to destroy her son and keep him from becoming God's instrument. After twenty-two years, during which he faced death again and again, God's individualized, providential circumstances finally brought him to Christ, answering his mother's persevering prayers."[6]

As I read John Newton's biography, I thought about how God honored the prayers of his mother. She was alive to pray for him for only seven years, but those seven years of prayer were effective. He ran from God for twenty-two years, but he couldn't outrun his mother's prayers. After conversion he served God for forty-four years, twice as long. And his influence continues as millions have sung "Amazing Grace" in churches, under tents, and in homes around the world.

THE MOTHER WHO IMPACTED CHINA

One mother faithful in her prayer closet can bring a Christian influence to a country that for centuries has been in darkness.

Ni Kwei-tseng, born in China in 1869, became Mrs. Charles Jones Soong at age seventeen. Mrs. Soong had six children, four of whom grew to be highly distinguished public servants in Chinese history. Her daughter Mayling married General Chiang Kai-shek. Her second daughter, Chingling, married Sun Yat-sen, father of the Nationalist Republic of China and described as the "George Washington of the Chinese people." Her son T. V. Soong served as finance and foreign minister of China, and, like his sisters, worked throughout his life for the "betterment of the Chinese people."[7]

Mrs. Soong's fervent prayer life was a model to her children. She rose at dawn each day and spent hours with the Lord. Kneeling in a third-story prayer room, she didn't just take her concerns and desires for her own children to God but also her dreams and burdens for her nation. Her daughter said, "Asking God was not a matter of spending five minutes to ask Him to bless...and grant her request. It meant waiting on God for His leading."[8]

Because of her prayers and Christian witness, Mrs. Soong was called "China's Great Christian Mother." She ministered to the poor, the orphans, and the lost while passing a legacy of prayer and dependence on God to her children. Gathering her family for regular prayer and Bible reading, her highest aim was that they walk in the truth of the Bible, in the love of God and His wisdom. Because of her prayers, her son-in-law, President Chiang Kai-shek, became a Christian also. After she died, her children impacted thousands of Chinese people with the gospel and the witness of their own godly lives, through establishing missions, schools, orphanages, and serving in the Chinese government.

LEGACIES OF PRAYER

Susanna Wesley, a name familiar to most of us, is one of my favorite praying moms in history, and there is much we can learn from her. Of the nineteen children born to her between 1690 and 1709, only nine lived to adulthood. After her ninth child, Susanna decided no longer to set aside one hour for devotions and prayer, but two! Those who knew her attributed her spiritual legacy of courage and peace to her time with God each day.

Susanna didn't have an easy life. Their first rectory was a mud hut; she was married to a difficult man; their family home burned not once but twice, destroying almost everything; she faced mounting financial problems because of her husband's debts. Yet her strength was in God, and her purpose was clear—to raise children whose lives would glorify Christ.

Susanna trained her children strictly, teaching them six hours every day in their home school, but she knew their spiritual maturity would come from divine help. Her biography describes how she would tuck her children in bed each night and lift her candle to gaze upon each face. As she did so, she prayed that God would enable her to so inspire her children that they could be used by Him to change the world.

Her son John became a powerful preacher, both in England and the colonies, and founded the Methodist Movement. His sermons spread throughout England in the renewal fires of the Holy Spirit. Her son Charles, also a powerful preacher, wrote many beautiful hymns which are sung in churches even today.[9]

A PRAYER OF DEDICATION

When we dedicate our children to God and His work on the earth, and release them into His hands, who knows how God may use their lives? Patricia St. John, one of the first women to minister in Morocco and North Africa, and the author of children's classics such as *Treasures in the Snow,* tells in her autobiography how her mother's prayers influenced her destiny:

"From our very earliest years I think there were unseen, unrecognized forces at work in our young lives,"[10] she says. Their family had arrived in England after the end of World War I when fervor for missionary work was strong. Prominent Christian women held meetings in their homes to raise funds for the China Inland Mission and other Asian evangelistic efforts. It was fashionable for women moved by the appeal to drop their jewels, pearls, and money into the collection plates at the close of the meetings.

At one such gathering, Patricia's mother, a poor evangelist's wife, "sat, rather miserable, at the back and realized that she was out of place. She had nothing to give. Then almost like a voice came the thought, 'What is the most precious thing you possess?'

"'My three children,' she replied. Her heart lifted, and she walked boldly to the front and offered her three babies to God for the mission field. And that, in those days, was no small sacrifice; there were no short-termers, few furloughs, and so many died. Yet she secretly held to her resolve." In the margin of her Bible, beside Psalm 84:3 she wrote, "Only yielded up in the place of sacrifice are they perfectly safe."[11] Although her mother told her nothing of her prayers until she was an adult, Patricia remembered the day she and her brother, at ages twelve and thirteen, were swinging in a beech tree and decided they would be missionaries together when they grew up.

Patricia trained as a nurse and served in a hospital in England during World War II. After the war she was a missionary in Tangier from 1949 until 1976 (much of that time working with her brother, the director of the hospital). She also influenced generations of children with the books that she wrote.

Another great evangelist and author, R. A. Torrey, tells of the impact of his mother's prayers when he was "about as near eternal damnation as anyone gets. I had one foot over the brink and was trying to get the other one over."[12] He wasn't seeking God, wasn't in church or Sunday school (which should encourage those of us whose kids aren't attending youth group!), and didn't have the slightest thought of being converted.

Torrey was awakened in the middle of the night one night and was converted to Christ within five minutes. "I thought no human being had anything to do with it, but I had forgotten my mother's prayers.... There are few converted in this world in any other way than in connection with someone's prayers," Torrey concludes.[13]

IT'S TIME TO COME OUT OF THE CLOSET

While having time to pray in seclusion—where we can really concentrate and remain focused—is essential, it's also important to come out of our prayer closets to pray *with* our children. As when mates pray together, we may learn more about what's on someone's heart by listening to and partnering in their prayers than in any other way.

Charles Stanley often shares that the best way for children to see and desire an intimate relationship with Christ is by observing their parents' prayer life. That's because he attributes much of his own hunger to know and trust God to the godly influence of his mother. As he was growing up, each night he and his mom knelt together beside his bed and prayed. They thanked God for His provision and protection and took their everyday concerns to Him.

Later, as a teenager, when Stanley worked the night shift at a local mill, he would arrive home after midnight. His mother would have a meal waiting for him, and they would take time to kneel together at his bedside, praying for God's guidance and counsel for his life. Her prayers not only influenced his ministry and his becoming a man of prayer, but they impacted his relationship with his children as well.[14]

PUTTING FEET TO OUR PRAYERS

Maybe, like me, you're a little intimidated when you read that Mrs. Charles Jones Soong prayed three hours a day or that Susanna Wesley began to pray two hours a day when she became a mother of nine children. Perhaps the following suggestion will help.

Pray a classic prayer. When I get frustrated trying to express my needs and feelings to God, struggle with wandering thoughts, or just run out of ideas on how to pray, I find it helpful to pray a prayer written by someone else. Prayers of godly people in Christian history can be an inspiration just as biblical prayers like The Lord's Prayer, David's confession in Psalm 51, and Paul's prayers for the Ephesians have been for centuries.

When I read the prayers of Hannah Whitall Smith or Amy Carmichael or countless others, my heart resonates with theirs. It reminds me of what 1 Corinthians 10:13 says, "No test or temptation that comes your way is beyond the course of what others have had to face. All you need to remember is that God will never let you down; he'll never let you be pushed past your limit; he'll always be there to help you come through it" (THE MESSAGE). Their prayers can be a springboard to our own communication with God, and most amazing of all, can sometimes express what's on our hearts even more clearly than we can.

Here are some of my favorites:

Holy Spirit, think through me till your ideas are my ideas.

AMY CARMICHAEL

On Thy breast, I pillow my head. O Jesus, Lover of my soul,
Thy will be done in me.
Give me faith to trust where I cannot know.
Give me greater love and desire in prayer
for all for whom I daily intercede.
Give me faith to appropriate the grace I need to continue
by prayer, by effort, by giving, to do Thy will.
O Lord, overcome, for the battle is Thine.
Forgive my doubts and save me from my fears.
Whatever my struggle, enable me to be helpful,
rather than a hindrance to Thy cause.
I love Thee.... Thy will be done. Amen.

CHARLES SPURGEON

Lord, I'm Yours, Yours wholly and Yours forever!
I am Yours by the purchase of Your blood and I give myself to
you now
as a living sacrifice—body, soul and spirit—to be as clay in your
hands.
I give you my heart, Lord, to love only what You love,
to hate what You hate, to endure all things, to suffer long and be kind,
to be not so easily provoked. To think no evil, not to seek my
own—
help me, oh my God!
I give you my mind to be wholly devoted to Your service
and perfectly under Your control, to think only those thoughts
that will please You,
to devise only such plans as You suggest....
To bring every thought to the obedience of Christ,
Help me, oh my God!

HANNAH WHITALL SMITH, *DIARIES*

Thank you, Lord Jesus,
that you will be our hiding place,
whatever happens.

CORRIE TEN BOOM[15]

O Lord, Jesus Christ,
who art as the shadow of a great rock in a weary land,
who beholdest thy weak creatures
weary of labour, weary of pleasure,
weary of hope deferred, weary of self;
in thine abundant compassion
and fellow feeling with us,
and unutterable tenderness,
bring us, we pray thee,
unto thy rest.

CHRISTINA ROSSETTI[16]

Through prayer you will discover
that God has a magnetic attracting quality!...
The Lord naturally draws you more and more
toward Himself.

MADAME GUYON

CHAPTER SEVENTEEN

THE PRAYER THAT CHANGES THE PRAY-ER

But we all, with unveiled face
beholding as in a mirror the glory of the Lord,
are being transformed into the same image
from glory to glory,
just as from the Lord, the Spirit.
2 CORINTHIANS 3:18

We've looked backward to mothers in history who prayed and trusted God with their concerns. We've looked outward to see how God is working in colleges, communities, and even other nations as mothers pray to change school situations, to transform their children's lives, to bring home prodigals, to restore physical and emotional health, and especially to bring salvation to the lost. But we have one other direction we must look, possibly the most critical direction. We must look inward to see how prayer affects us as pray-ers.

"Prayer changes us and therein lies its glory and its purpose," said Hannah Hurnard. What has struck me—through my own prayer journey, through my prayer groups, and through hearing other women's experiences, many of which are recounted in this book—is how much the pray-er is transformed. Certainly in the process of researching and writing this book, God has worked within me.

Hearing the stories of how God has met women in their crises and everyday lives has greatly encouraged me and refreshed and renewed my own prayer life. I have several longstanding issues I've prayed about many, many times, just as you may have, and from time to time I find myself getting weary. But a new hope has infused my petitions, and my faith and perseverance have been increased by hearing of God's faithfulness. Their stories have also prompted me to action. I was so inspired by what is happening with college kids and on campuses as mothers pray for them that I started a new college moms prayer group.

But as encouraging as these outward changes are, I was reminded over and over that even when outward situations are not resolved, the Lord can bring peace and change us on the inside. Prayer brings us to the point that no matter what turmoil or storm rages around us we can be still and know that He is God. As we enter into the process of prayer—with our praise, confessions, thanksgiving, and intercession—our perspective changes. Praise raises our eyes from the problem to the Victor, so that we're looking "from the top" rather than from beneath the load, as Amy Carmichael says.

As we regularly enter into confession, the "Clean Heart" principle operates powerfully.[1] We want God to hear our prayers for our children, and yet we know, "If I regard wickedness in my heart, the Lord will not hear me" (Psalm 66:18). So as we come into God's presence and ask Him to create in us clean hearts and renew a right spirit within us, He shows us those dark areas that need repentance and cleansing. We confess whatever He shows us—pride, control, anger, critical words—and receive God's forgiveness. As this becomes a moment-by-moment habit, we walk with a clean heart and keep shorter accounts with people and with God. This aspect of prayer alone brings major transformation in our lives.

A GRACE-FILLED RELEASE

Another amazing inner change I've found is that as we pray for our children, a supernatural grace fills us in the releasing process. I say *supernatural* because it's not "natural" for moms to let go; we're created for nurturing. We've all heard that old advice to give our children "roots and wings," but it's easier said than done! Our strong mother-love can lead us to become controlling or overprotective, holding our kids too close and hindering their growth to maturity.

But through prayer the releasing process is filled with grace—an ease, an acceptance, even joy—instead of clinging, control, and sorrow. As we pray for our young people, we find we can still have a great influence in their lives, no matter how old they are. Prayer helps us keep in balance what is our part, what is our child's part, and what is God's part. It helps us let God work in their hearts as they grow up, trusting Him to protect them. Then our prayers become truly the wind beneath their wings.

I was vividly reminded of how this letting-go grace operates when my friend Pat told me of her son Tea Jay's terrible accident. One September night riding his bike home from work, he was struck by a hit-and-run driver. His crumpled body and bike were found in a ditch, and he was in critical condition.

Arriving at the emergency room, Pat was told his neck was fractured around the C-4 vertebrae but was still intact, so there was no paralysis. He lay squirming on a backboard in a pool of blood from his ear to his knees, his hip cut to the bone and signs of internal injuries. The ER nurse had to hold Tea Jay's head, and his arms and legs had to be restrained by heavy straps all night because he was thrashing in and out of consciousness.

As Pat looked at the restraints, she knew she had a decision to make. Tea Jay was a rock climber, cross-country bike rider, and risktaker who loved adventure. One of her greatest fears had long been that something like this would happen. "Just like those physical restraints, I knew I could try to restrain him for the rest of his life from the adventurous activities he loves, or I could release him to the Lord's care and trust Him. I knew I didn't want to tie him down like those straps, so I released Tea Jay to the Lord—an act of faith and, ultimately, freeing to us both."

After a stay in the ICU and serious complications, her son recovered and resumed his normal activities. That spring he rode his bicycle from Oklahoma to Colorado to work at a Young Life Camp, leading high school kids up a mountain on six-day expeditions. That summer he climbed Mount Rainier, biked to Yosemite for rock climbing, and later set off on a bicycle trip.

Although the family was grateful for the many ways God had protected Tea Jay and restored his health, how did Pat avoid being overwhelmed with fear for his safety? By consciously releasing Tea Jay that night in the ER and covering him in prayer on his journeys, she has been filled with peace about her son; she has released him with grace and faith. "God doesn't call us to a life of fear, and I desire not to live in fear but in peace because He protects, not only Tea Jay but all my family members. God is still sovereign," she says.

FUELED BY HOPE

Paul must have had moms in mind when he advised not to be weary in well doing. Sometimes we feel as if we're in a dark cave without a flashlight, and when a situation goes on and on without relief or resolution, we even experience the "hope deferred [which] makes the heart sick" that Proverbs 13:12 refers to. But when we can glimpse what God is doing, it fuels and encourages us.

Over the years of praying for her three older sons, my friend Peggy has felt the sickness of hope deferred more times than she'd like to remember. But she also rejoices over the times God has graciously stilled the aching of her heart and gently re-centered her hope in Him alone.

One such occasion came at the conclusion of Josh's freshman year of college. Although this son had participated in many family worship times as a teen, he now was "headstrong and headlong in an affair with the world." Her concerns caused her to cry out to God one spring day in deep perplexity of spirit. She poured out her fears, her unrest, and her grief, and she prayed that the Lord would pour out His Spirit and lead him to deep repentance. She also asked if somehow He would let her know He was at work in Josh's life.

That very day God answered Peggy through her son's own words. Unknown to her, he had planned to take her to dinner for Mother's Day. He opened up to her that evening in a way he never had before, sharing some of his deepest thoughts. As he related them to her, it was obvious that the Holy Spirit had been continuously at work behind all that she saw on the surface. Her heart melted at God's graciousness in giving her a glimpse into His faithful work. Although Josh told her he wasn't yet ready to yield himself completely to God, God had answered her that day, reassuring her that we do not pray in vain.

OUT OF DEPRESSION INTO PRAISE

"I have sunk in deep mire, and there is no foothold; I have come into deep waters, and a flood overflows me. I am weary with my crying.... My eyes fail while I wait for my God," says the psalmist (Psalm 69:2–3). The way out of such a depression is long and arduous. But many women have found that entering into a regular weekly prayer time with other women can bring them out of depression and open up windows of strength and opportunity.

When Deanna moved to Seattle, she was in a severe state of depression. Because of his job, her husband had already moved, but she and their two young children had to stay behind to sell the house. By the time they got back together as a family, they'd been separated for most of the last eighteen months, and he was like a stranger to the kids. Their marriage was struggling, and she was exhausted from parenting two little ones alone. When her oldest child entered the Seattle public schools, Deanna heard about Moms In Touch from another mother.

"I was a basket case at that point," she says. "I was deeply depressed, and these three moms and I would get together for an hour to pray for our children. Then afterward they'd pray for me and send me back out the door."

The discipline of praying for others during that weekly prayer time helped her to get into the presence of God, and God began healing her depression and gradually lifting her heavy burdens as she was obedient to pray for her children, the school, and teachers. At the end of the year, she was asked to lead the group. "I can't lead," she protested, but the leader persisted. It took Deanna a week to prepare the five-minute devotional for that first meeting, but she grew and became more self-confident, eventually serving as an area coordinator and as part of the six-member Washington State MITI team.

She still suffered bouts of depression at times, however. At one very low point, she called Diane, another coordinator, and asked, "How do I make it through this?"

"You must learn how to praise the Lord, honey," Diane counseled.

Deanna felt so depressed she couldn't form a prayer or praise God, couldn't generate anything out of herself, so she began to listen to praise music and search the Scriptures.

When she read Habakkuk 3:17–19—that even if the fig tree doesn't blossom or the field produces no fruit or food, "I will exult in the Lord"—she turned the corner, understanding that her praise couldn't be based on her feelings but on who God is. She decided whatever happened she would praise Him. As she became more thankful, she became less angry. The confession time of her prayer group helped her keep current on her confession and receive God's cleansing. Gradually her smile reappeared; six months later, her laugh was back, and then the song in her heart returned.

When the state coordinator stepped down, Deanna was asked to take her place. In those few years, God had prepared her by working at her husband's company as an office manager, where she learned techniques she'd need to train and coordinate area leaders and MITI groups. Although she has continued to face difficulties, she has the support of other praying women. And God has lifted her up out of the pit of depression, strengthened her from the inside, and set her feet upon the Rock.

A DIVINE EXCHANGE

Jesus' first miracle was changing water into wine at a wedding feast. In fact, Jesus always brought change, wherever He went. He made the sick well, forgave sins, sought out those shunned by the Jews and the established religious and social order, overturned the tables of moneychangers in the temple, and elevated the lowly to places of honor. In a similar way when we come to Him in prayer, He makes a divine exchange. Anxiety and fear are changed to faith and greater reliance on God. Heaviness and depression are replaced with a spirit of praise. Our complaining or fretting is turned into thanksgiving. Despair and discouragement are transformed into hope. Increasingly our hearts are cleansed and altered as we realize we've got to be right before God and others to come into the throne room with our requests.

"To pray is to change. This is a great grace," says Richard Foster. "How good of God to provide a path whereby our lives can be taken over by love and joy and peace and patience and kindness and goodness and faithfulness and gentleness and self control."[2] What a wondrous thing it is when God changes us! For the most important thing that happens in prayer is that our eyes are riveted on Him, the Giver, instead of the gifts we ask for, and we discover that no matter when or how our prayers are answered, He is our reward.

"Prayer enlarges the heart until it is capable of containing God's gift of himself," said Mother Teresa. Prayer, in fact, is a growing, ongoing love relationship with God through the Father, Son, and Holy Spirit.[3] As the Lord Jesus Christ becomes the focus of our lives, the eyes of our hearts are opened, and we see more clearly His faithfulness and His lovingkindness. "Whenever a man turns to the Lord, the veil is taken away," or as The Message says, "Nothing between us and God, our faces shining with the brightness of his face" (2 Corinthians 3:16). As we walk with Him, talk with Him, and behold Him daily in our lives, transformation comes. We are drawn closer to Him the more we come into His presence to intercede for others—and in His presence is fullness of joy.

The Lord promises, "Then you will call upon Me and come and pray to Me, and I will listen to you. And you will seek Me and find Me, when you search for Me with all your heart" (Jeremiah 29:12–13). When we find Him—our Father, Mighty God, the King of kings who is our Savior and Friend—our hearts can rest.

And when we get to heaven, we will then truly know all that He did through our prayers.

Lord, I pray that You will encourage and strengthen us.
Give us a strong and widened heart
to believe what a mighty influence our prayers can exert.
Grant us the grace to persistently, earnestly,
and expectantly continue praying and waiting upon You.
Help us to see everything in the overriding light that You are Love,
and give us the faith to believe that as we seek You,
we will find You—
the God of All Hope!

In Your Son's Name. Amen.

NOTES

CHAPTER TWO

1. The Living Bible

2. Ibid.

3. E. M. Bounds, *The Possibilities of Prayer* (Springdale, Pa.: Whitaker House, 1994), 87.

4. Anne Morrow Lindbergh, *Gift from the Sea* (N.Y.: Random House, 1955), 28.

5. Judson Cornwall, *Praying the Scriptures: Communicating with God in His Own Words* (Lake Mary, Fla.: Creation House, 1988), 15.

CHAPTER THREE

1. Richard Foster, *Prayer: Finding the Heart's True Home* (N.Y.: HarperCollins Publishers, 1992), 11.

2. Ibid., 12.

3. My thanks to Barbara Sorrell, a Tulsa, Oklahoma, mom, for sharing with me her understanding of praying through the developmental stages of a child's life.

CHAPTER FOUR

1. Catherine Marshall, *Adventures in Prayer* (N.Y.: Ballantine Books, 1975), 64.

2. O. Hallesby, *Prayer* (Minneapolis: Augsburg Press, 1994; original ed., 1931), 18–19, 27.

3. Ibid., 19.

4. Ibid., 20.

CHAPTER FIVE

1. Rosalind Rinker, *Prayer: Conversing with God* (Grand Rapids: Zondervan Publishing House, 1959), 43.

2. Ibid., 42.

3. Fern Nichols, *Heart to Heart* 7, no. 4 (Winter 1995): 1.

CHAPTER SIX

1. Cornwall, *Praying the Scriptures*, 72.

2. Edith Deen, *Great Women of the Christian Faith* (Westwood, N.J.: Barbour and Company, 1959), 23.

3. Ibid., 23.

4. "Pushing Inward," *Christian History* 15, no. 4: 10–11.

CHAPTER SEVEN

1. Marshall, *Adventures in Prayer*, 51.

2. Ibid., 48.

3. Ibid., 49.

4. Genesis 22:14

5. Exodus 15:26

6. Exodus 17:15

7. Ezekiel 48:35

8. After incubating a few of my own prayers for my teenagers, I came across the idea of cutting out the request in the shape of an egg in Catherine Marshall's wonderful little book *Adventures in Prayer,* (p. 47), an idea suggested to her by Dr. Glenn Clark's writings. He said that "part of our problem in praying for our children is the time lag, the necessary slow maturation of our prayers. But that's the way of God's rhythm in nature." I highly recommend this idea for those of us "in waiting."

CHAPTER EIGHT

1. *Webster's Seventh New Collegiate Dictionary,* s.v. "revival."

2. Bill Bright, *The Coming Revival: America's Call to Fast, Pray, and "Seek God's Face"* (Orlando: NewLife Publications, 1995), 82–86.

3. R. A. Torrey, *How to Pray* (Springdale, Pa.: Whitaker House, 1983), 96–105.

4. Andrew Murray, *The Ministry of Intercessory Prayer* (Minneapolis: Bethany House Publishers, 1981), 110.

5. Dan Coats, "America's Youth: A Crisis of Character," *IMPRIMIS* 20, no. 9 (September 1991): 1.

6. Daniel R. Levine, "Drugs Are Back—Big Time," *Reader's Digest,* February 1996, 71–76.

7. Coats, *IMPRIMIS,* 1.

8. Bright, *The Coming Revival,* 34.

9. Lamentations 2:19

10. "Nashville Students Claim Suburban Schools for Jesus with Daily Prayer," *Charisma,* November 1996, 31–32.

11. Wesley L. Duewel, *Mighty Prevailing Prayer* (Grand Rapids: Zondervan Publishing House, 1990), 257.

12. Quoted in Duewel, *Mighty Prevailing Prayer,* 135.

13. Oswald Chambers, *My Utmost for His Highest,* special updated ed., ed. James Reimann (Nashville, Tenn.: Discovery House, Thomas Nelson Publishers, 1995), November 7 entry.

14. Duewel, *Mighty Prevailing Prayer,* 18.

CHAPTER NINE

1. Marshall, *Adventures in Prayer,* 48.

2. Duewel, *Mighty Prevailing Prayer,* 152.

3. Andrew Murray, *With Christ in the School of Prayer,* (Springdale, Pa.: Whitaker House, 1981), 119.

CHAPTER TEN

1. Dr. Richard Stevens and Dr. Jay Kesler, *Focus on the Family* broadcast, February 1997.

2. Gary Bauer, *Family Research Council Newsletter,* 3 March 1997, 2.

3. Lydia Harris, "Finding Another College Mom," material sent to those interested in starting or participating in a college MITI group.

CHAPTER ELEVEN

1. Evelyn Christenson, "Intercessory Prayer," vol. 17 of Focus on the Family's *Pastor to Pastor* tape series.

2. T. Davis Bunn, *The Quilt* (Minneapolis: Bethany House Publishers, 1993), 90–91.

CHAPTER TWELVE

1. Dennis Jernigan, "I Long for the Day," *I Belong to Jesus,* vol. 2 © Shepherd's Heart Music, 1993.

CHAPTER THIRTEEN

1. Torrey, *How to Pray,* 13.

2. Duewel, *Mighty Prevailing Prayer,* 132.

3. Ibid.

CHAPTER FOURTEEN

1. The name of the country and actual names of the people involved in the story cannot be used for the safety of these pastors and sisters in the Lord.

2. Amy Carmichael, *Edges of His Ways: Selections for Daily Readings* (Fort Washington, Pa.: Christian Literature Crusade, 1975), 21.

CHAPTER FIFTEEN

1. Lucien Aigner, *What Prayer Can Do* (Garden City, N.Y.: Doubleday and Company, Inc., 1953), 22–23.

2. Amy Carmichael, *Candles in the Dark* (Ft. Washington, Pa.: Christian Literature Crusade, 1981), 35.

CHAPTER SIXTEEN

1. David Barton, *The Bulletproof George Washington* (Aledo, Tex.: WallBuilder Press, 1990), 23.

2. From a sermon by Dennis Baw, Pastor of the Glenview Baptist Church in Ft. Worth, Texas.

3. Barton, *The Bulletproof George Washington,* 49.

4. Ibid., 47.

5. Catherine Swift et. al., *John Newton* (Minneapolis: Bethany House Publishers, 1991), 94–95.

6. Duewel, *Mighty Prevailing Prayer,* 151–52.

7. Deen, *Great Women*, 275–77.

8. Ibid., 277.

9. Wendy Leifeld, *Mothers of the Saints: Portraits of Ten Mothers of the Saints and Three Saints Who Were Mothers* (Ann Arbor, Mich.: Servant Publications, 1991), 132.

10. Patricia St. John, *An Ordinary Woman's Extraordinary Faith: The Autobiography of Patricia St. John* (Wheaton, Ill.: Harold Shaw Publishers, 1993), 78.

11. Ibid., 79.

12. Torrey, *How to Pray,* 20.

13. Ibid., 19–20.

14. Charles Stanley, *In Touch Ministries* letter, (May 1992): 1–2.

15. Corrie ten Boom, "The Hiding Place," *Eerdmans Book of Famous Prayers* (Grand Rapids: William B. Eerdmans Publishing Company, 1983), 88.

16. Christina Rosetti, "In Weariness," *Eerdmans Book of Famous Prayers,* 78.

CHAPTER SEVENTEEN

1. Cindy Jacobs, *Possessing the Gates of the Enemy: A Handbook on Militant Intercession* (Grand Rapids: Chosen/Baker Book House, 1991), 40–47.

2. Foster, *Prayer,* 6.

3. Ibid.

RECOMMENDED BOOKS ON PRAYER

Bounds, E. M. *The Possibilities of Prayer.* Springdale, Pa.: Whitaker House, 1994. This book goes into the heart of prayer. In it, Bounds shares the wonders of God's power in prayer, prayer in history, the relationship between God's provision, providence, and miracles through prayer.

Bright, Bill. *The Coming Revival: American's Call to Fast, Pray, and "Seek God's Face."* Orlando: NewLife Publications, 1995. This book is a call to the repentance and prayer needed to bring revival to our nation and personal revival to our lives. It includes secrets of a successful prayer life, ways to prepare for and undertake a fast, and how to lead a congregation in a time of prayer and fasting.

Christenson, Evelyn. *What Happens When Women Pray.* Wheaton, Ill.: Victor Books, 1975, 1991. With practical teachings from prayer seminars the author conducted all over the world, this is a down-to-earth, biblical book for personal study and includes many helps on praying with groups.

Dean, Jennifer. *The Praying Life: Living beyond Your Limits.* Birmingham, Ala.: New Hope, 1993. The author shares what she has learned in her quest to pray effectively and to make prayer the center and driving force of the whole Christian life.

Duewel, Wesley L. *Mighty Prevailing Prayer.* Grand Rapids: Zondervan Publishing House, 1990. A comprehensive, motivational book on persistent, persevering prayer, militant prayer, and spiritual warfare. It is an excellent guide for how to pray more effectively and how to respond to God's call to intercession.

Foster, Richard. *Prayer: Finding the Heart's True Home.* N. Y.: HarperCollins Publishers, 1992. Foster writes a warm and personal, yet extremely insightful, book on prayer which leads the reader into the practice of prayer with the expectation of meeting a loving God. He also discusses some of the mysteries and difficulties in prayer.

Fuller, Cheri. *Trading Your Worry for Wonder.* Among other topics, this book discusses the role of prayer in dealing with anxieties and worries. Included at the back are questions for group discussion or personal reflection.

Hallesby, O. *Prayer.* Minneapolis: Augsburg Press, 1994, original ed., 1931. This classic book on prayer by a Norwegian prayer theologian includes secrets of effective prayer and difficulties and problems in prayer, and includes an excellent study guide.

Heald, Cynthia. *Becoming a Woman of Prayer: A Bible Study.* Colorado Springs: NavPress Publishing Group, 1996. With classic quotes on prayer, thought-provoking reflections by the author, and suggested memory verses, this is an excellent resource for personal or small-group Bible study.

Hybels, Bill. *Too Busy Not to Pray: Slowing Down to Be with God.* Downers Grove, Ill.: InterVarsity Press, 1988. Hybels covers the basics of prayer, the ACTS model, the importance of listening to God, and how to listen.

Jacobs, Cindy. *Possessing the Gates of the Enemy: A Handbook on Militant Intercession.* Grand Rapids: Chosen/Baker Book House, 1991. Whether you are a beginning pray-er or an experienced intercessor, you'll find this a helpful book on spiritual warfare and intercession.

Lockyer, Herbert. *All the Prayers of the Bible.* Grand Rapids, Mich.: Zondervan Publishing House, 1959. This is a classic and comprehensive book on the multitude of prayers in the Old and New Testaments. It includes a Scripture index where the reader can find different kinds of prayers in the Bible, including prayers for times of peril, fear, gratitude, or distress.

Marshall, Catherine. *Adventures in Prayer.* N. Y.: Ballantine Books, 1975. Originally published in the 1950s, this is one of my favorite Catherine Marshall books as she shares her personal journey and "adventures" in prayer.

Murray, Andrew. *The Ministry of Intercessory Prayer.* Minneapolis: Bethany House Publishers, 1981. This is a practical, classic manual on intercessory prayer with prayer motivators and a gold mine of biblical instruction. Included in the latter part of the book is a thirty-day study course in the practice of intercession.

Murray, Andrew. *With Christ in the School of Prayer.* Springdale, Pa.: Whitaker House, 1981. One of the best-loved and best-known prayer classics, the book shares how to prepare for the highest calling Christ gave the Church—the call to intercessory prayer.

Nichols, Fern. *Moms In Touch International: Mothers Meeting to Pray for Their Children and Schools.* Poway, Calif.: Moms In Touch International, 1987. A book that enables the reader to start or participate in a Moms In Touch group, it includes a personal testimony by Nichols; prayer suggestions for children, teachers, and schools; the Four Steps of Prayer; scriptural prayers; and ideas on ministering to school staff and faculty.

Rinker, Rosalind. *Prayer: Conversing with God.* Grand Rapids: Zondervan Publishing House, 1959. One of the best books on the dynamics of conversational prayer, it contains insights and practical helps on praying with groups.

Torrey, R. A. *Prayer.* Springdale, Pa.: Whitaker House, 1983. This dynamic book shows how prayer is vital to our faith and how we can pray more effectively when we understand God's methods of hearing and answering prayer. The topics include praying according to God's will, abiding in Christ, and praying for revival.

Word Ministries, Inc. *Prayers that Avail Much: An Intercessor's Handbook of Scriptural Prayers.* Tulsa, Okla.: Harrison House, 1980. This is a handbook for scriptural praying arranged topically by prayers for personal concerns, intercessory prayers for the needs of family, others, and the world.

ABOUT THE AUTHOR

Cheri Fuller is an inspirational speaker and the award-winning author of more than twenty-five books including *When Couples Pray: The Little-Known Secret to Lifelong Happiness in Marriage, When Children Pray,* and *When Families Pray,* a unique devotional for parents and kids. *When Mothers Pray* is also published in Spanish, Portuguese, and Norwegian. With a Master's degree in English Literature, Cheri's messages, magazine articles, and books provide encouragement to women throughout the U.S. and other countries.

Cheri is founder of Families Pray USA and author of the Internet columns "Mothering By Heart" on www.cherifuller.com, which offers inspiration, ideas, and encouragement for moms and www.familiesprayusa.org, which includes stories, resources, and tips on praying for and with our children.

Cheri frequently speaks at women's conferences and events and has been a guest on hundreds of radio programs such as *Focus on the Family, Moody's Prime Time America, ParentTalk, NBC Radio News,* and others. She's a contributing editor for *Today's Christian Woman* magazine and *Pray!* magazine and has written frequently for *Family Circle, Focus on the Family, Guideposts, Decision, Parentlife,* and other magazines.

Cheri leads a College Moms In Touch prayer group and a children's prayer team. She and her husband, Holmes, have three grown and married children, two grandchildren, and live in Oklahoma.

To contact Cheri for speaking engagements:

Speak Up Speaker Services

(810)982-0898, voice or (810)987-4163, fax

Speakupinc@aol.com

1614 Edison Shores Place • Port Huron, MI • 48060-3374